access to history

BRITAIN *and the* EUROPEAN POWERS *1815–65*

Michael Byrne

Hodder & Stoughton

A MEMBER OF THE HODDER HEADLINE GROUP

Some other titles in the series:

Britain and the European Powers, 1865–1914
Robert Pearce   ISBN 0 340 64327 7

Great Britain and the Irish Question, 1800–1922
Paul Adelman   ISBN 0 340 54646 8

Whigs, Radicals and Liberals, 1815-1914
Duncan Watts   ISBN 0 340 62703 4

The British Empire, 1815–1914
Frank McDonough   ISBN 0 340 59376 8

Orders: please contact Bookpoint Ltd, 39 Milton Park, Abingdon, Oxon
OX14 4TD. Telephone: (44) 01235 400414, Fax: (44) 01235 400454. Lines
are open from 9.00 - 6.00, Monday to Saturday, with a 24 hour message
answering service. Email address: orders@bookpoint.co.uk

British Library Cataloguing in Publication Data

A catalogue for this title is available from the British Library

ISBN 0 340 67926 3

First published 1998

Impression number	10	9	8	7	6	5	4	3	2	1
Year			2002		2001		2000		1999	1998

Copyright © 1998 Michael Byrne

The cover illustration is a portrait of George Canning by Sir Thomas Lawrence
reproduced courtesy of the National Portrait Gallery, London.
Illustrations by Ian Foulis & Associates Ltd, Saltash
Typeset by Sempringham publishing services, Bedford
Printed in Great Britain for Hodder & Stoughton Educational, a division of Hodder
Headline Plc, 338 Euston Road, London NW1 3BH

Contents

Preface

To the general reader

Although the *Access to History* series has been designed with the needs of students studying the subject at higher examination levels very much in mind, it also has a great deal to offer the general reader. The main body of the text (i.e. ignoring the 'Study Guides' at the ends of chapters) forms a readable and yet stimulating survey of a coherent topic as studied by historians. However, each author's aim has not merely been to provide a clear explanation of what happened in the past (to interest and inform): it has also been assumed that most readers wish to be stimulated into thinking further about the topic and to form opinions of their own about the significance of the events that are described and discussed (to be challenged). Thus, although no prior knowledge of the topic is expected on the reader's part, she or he is treated as an intelligent and thinking person throughout. The author tends to share ideas and possibilities with the reader, rather than passing on numbers of so-called 'historical truths'.

To the student reader

There are many ways in which the series can be used by students studying history at a higher level. It will, therefore, be worthwhile thinking about your own study strategy before you start your work on this book. Obviously, your strategy will vary depending on the aim you have in mind, and the time for study that is available to you.

If, for example, you want to acquire a general overview of the topic in the shortest possible time, the following approach will probably be the most effective:

1. Read Chapter 1 and think about its contents.
2. Read the 'Making notes' section at the end of Chapter 2 and decide whether it is necessary for you to read this chapter.
3. If it is, read the chapter, stopping at each heading to note down the main points that have been made.
4. Repeat stage 2 (and stage 3 where appropriate) for all the other chapters.

If, however, your aim is to gain a thorough grasp of the topic, taking however much time is necessary to do so, you may benefit from carrying out the same procedure with each chapter, as follows:

1. Read the chapter as fast as you can, and preferably at one sitting.
2. Study the flow diagram at the end of the chapter, ensuring that you understand the general 'shape' of what you have just read.

3. Read the 'Making notes' section (and the 'Answering essay questions' section, if there is one) and decide what further work you need to do on the chapter. In particularly important sections of the book, this will involve reading the chapter a second time and stopping at each heading to think about (and to write a summary of) what you have just read.
4. Attempt the 'Source-based questions' section. It will sometimes be sufficient to think through your answers, but additional understanding will often be gained by forcing yourself to write them down.

When you have finished the main chapters of the book, study the 'Further Reading' section and decide what additional reading (if any) you will do on the topic.

This book has been designed to help make your studies both enjoyable and successful. If you can think of ways in which this could have been done more effectively, please write to tell me. In the meantime, I hope that you will gain greatly from your study of History.

Keith Randell

Acknowledgements

The Publishers would like to thank the following for permission to reproduce material in this volume:

Adam & Charles Black for extracts from *Britain and Europe: Pitt to Churchill, 1793-1940* by James Joll (1961); Macmillan Publishers for an extract from *Castlereagh* by CJ Bartlett (1966); Constable for an extract from *Lord Palmerston* by Jasper Ridley; Cassell for an extract from 'The Gathering Storm' from *The Second World War vol.1* by Winston Churchill (1950).

The Publishers would like to thank the following for permission to reproduce the following copyright illustrations:
Cover - courtesy of the National Portrait Gallery, London. Page 49, © The British Museum; page 100, Punch Picture Library.

Every effort has been made to trace and acknowledge ownership of copyright. The Publishers will be glad to make suitable arrangements with copyright holders whom it has not been possible to contact.

1 Introduction: British Foreign Policy - Principles and Practice

The year 1815 marked a turning point in European history. At the battle of Waterloo in June of that year British forces under the command of the Duke of Wellington finally defeated the forces of France under Napoleon Bonaparte. It was the end of an era of French imperial domination against which Britain had fought for over two decades. The purpose of this book is to study the diplomatic relations between Britain and the other European powers in the fifty years which followed this momentous battle. The purpose of this opening chapter is to provide an understanding of the fundamental issues and circumstances which guided the way in which British governments responded to events in Europe, or in some instances elsewhere, over that period. In many ways Waterloo was not a turning point for Britain in quite the same way as it was for Europe, and one of the aims of this chapter is to show how important the long-term continuity of the basic elements of British foreign policy was in the period from 1815 to 1865.

1 The Principles of British Foreign Policy

In March 1936 Winston Churchill, who within a few years would be Prime Minister of Great Britain in the Second World War, was invited to address a private meeting of the Conservative MPs' Committee on Foreign Affairs. It was a time when British foreign policy in Europe generally, and towards Nazi Germany in particular, was becoming highly controversial. Churchill, a keen historian and devotee of foreign affairs, used the opportunity to deliver a classic interpretation of the fundamental principles of British foreign policy.

1   For four hundred years the foreign policy of England has been to oppose the strongest, most aggressive, most dominating Power on the Continent, and particularly to prevent the Low Countries [Belgium and Holland] falling into the hands of such a Power. Viewed in the light of
5   history, these four centuries of consistent purpose amid so many changes of names and facts, of circumstances and conditions, must rank as one of the most remarkable episodes which the records of any race, nation, State, or people can show. Moreover, on all occasions England [or Britain as it was from the early eighteenth century] took the more
10 difficult course. Faced by Philip II of Spain [in the second half of the sixteenth century], against Louis XIV [in the early eighteenth century], against Napoleon [in the early nineteenth century] ... against William II of Germany [in the First World War, 1914-18], it would have been easy and must have been very tempting to join with the stronger and share

15 the fruits of his conquest. However, we always took the harder course, joined with the less strong Powers, made a combination among them, and thus defeated and frustrated the Continental military tyrant, who-ever he was, whatever nation he led. Thus we preserved the liberties of Europe ... and emerged after ... terrible struggles with an ever-growing
20 fame and widening Empire, and with the Low Countries safely protected in their independence. Here is the wonderful unconscious tradition of British Foreign Policy ... Observe that the policy ... takes no account of which nation it is that seeks the overlordship of Europe. The question is nor whether it is Spain, or the French Monarchy, or the French Empire,
25 or the German Empire, or the Hitler regime. It has nothing to do with rulers or nations; it is concerned solely with whoever is the strongest or the potentially dominating tyrant ... It is a law of public policy which we are following, and not a mere expedient dictated by accidental circum-stances, or likes and dislikes, or any other sentiment.

Churchill's interpretation presents the principles of British foreign policy as a selfless pilgrimage of protection of the weak against tyranny; a high moral mission for the defence of freedom against oppression; a centuries-long crusade for liberty. Although in reality the fundamen-tals of British foreign policy were often less elevated, in its essentials Churchill's presentation comes down to two incontestable points: first, that it was British policy to oppose (if necessary by force), whichever was the greatest power in Europe at any given time and, secondly, that Britain sought to ensure that no such power was able to control the Low Countries. These aims were rooted in two specific concerns which can be generally defined as strategic and economic.

a) The Strategic Issue

As an island nation Britain's strategic vulnerability lay in the possi-bility of invasion by sea. The danger of this led Britain to secure control of Ireland, which in the hands of an enemy would pose a serious threat as a possible starting point for an assault. It also led to the emergence of the British Navy as a powerful weapon, designed to be strong enough to resist even a combination of other European navies if necessary. Although in 1588 the Spanish Armada had been defeated as much by luck and the elements as by English naval strength, in 1805 the Royal Navy had proved strong enough to defeat the combined fleets of France and Spain at the Battle of Trafalgar. The Low Countries, like Ireland, were a possible starting point for an invasion, offering access across the English Channel and either out into the North Sea or along the whole of the south coast of England. Since Britain could not reasonably expect to be able to impose British rule in the Low Countries (as was done in Ireland) their independence and neutrality was the best guarantee of British strategic interests.

b) The Economic Issue

As a trading nation Britain needed to be able to export her produce to European markets. As far back as the medieval period the export of raw wool had been a vital part of the economy; this had gradually been replaced in importance by the rise of the woollen cloth industry which had produced huge export revenues. During the eighteenth century the industrial revolution had seen the emergence of the cotton industry, the majority of the production of which went for export, as well as other manufacturing industries which came to dominate international trade. The Low Countries contained the major port of Antwerp, a gateway for trade routes into Europe. At various times since the middle ages enemies had tried to use denial of access to European markets as an economic weapon against Britain. The most recent example of this by 1815 was Napoleon Bonaparte's 'continental system' which had been an attempt at a reverse blockade to exclude British trade from continental Europe. The more powerful any given European nation became the greater the danger that it might seek to use its power to disrupt British trade. It followed that economic and strategic necessity led Britain to seek to prevent any one power in Europe from obtaining too strong a position. British naval supremacy was an economic weapon of offence as well as security against invasion in any such struggle against a continental enemy. Just as an enemy might seek to exclude Britain, so Britain could seek to maintain a blockade of major European ports in order to exert economic pressure on an opponent.

c) Liberty

What however of Churchill's claim that British foreign policy was an exercise in the preservation of liberty? This idea rests on the issue of 'constitutionalism' - i.e. the existence of a body of rules for the governing of a country which those who held power respected and followed. This contrasted with the idea of 'absolutism' in which an individual sovereign ruler held total power to make any decisions he or she chose without reference to any other authority apart (in theory at least) from that of Almighty God. In 1815 Britain had a constitution (based on a mixture of custom and statute law - it was not a written document) dating from 1689 under which the monarch shared political power with Parliament. One part of Parliament - the House of Lords - had its membership based on the hereditary aristocracy, whilst the other - the House of Commons - was made up of members who were elected by a limited number of the 'common people' who held their right to vote through a variety of qualifications. It was a feature of this varied electoral system, that in some types of constituency the vote was held by men of quite humble status.

This system was not in any sense democratic nor was it intended to be so. However, it did mean that British monarchs could not act without consultation and, indeed, could not rule at all without the cooperation of Parliament. The House of Commons, for example, controlled finance, holding the power to impose or withhold taxation and to decide on government expenditure. By convention (i.e. an unwritten agreement) even the House of Lords had no power in financial matters. However, financial matters aside, the House of Lords had full power to amend or veto any legislation. The monarch had an active political role in that he or she had the power to appoint and dismiss ministers and veto any legislation other than that concerning financial matters. But the monarch had to exercise these powers with caution because ministers had to be able to run the country through Parliament. This political system was a 'constitutional monarchy' in which the three sources of power - monarch, peers and members of the House of Commons (MPs) - acted as checks and balances against each other. The smooth conduct of government depended upon each acting responsibly and respecting the positions of the others. This system was unlike most of those in continental Europe which were based upon the absolutist principle and it was this constitutionalism which gave British foreign policy its claim to be based on higher principles than those of other European countries, because it was thought to protect the liberty of the individual citizen.

2 The Practice of British Foreign Policy

So far we have looked at the principles on which it can be argued that British foreign policy was based. However, principles are by definition abstract ideas and they have to be operated in practice in real situations. In this section we will examine the situations and constraints which affected the way in which foreign policy was conducted in actual practice.

a) The Role of the Foreign Secretary

The foreign secretary is the minister with direct political responsibility for running, on a day-to-day basis, the government department (the Foreign Office) which deals with Britain's relations with other countries. However, because of the supreme importance of this office - matters of war and peace can obviously hang on decisions made - the prime minister has always been seen as having a particular responsibility for it. In 1815, and for some time thereafter, the monarch was also seen as having a special role and responsibility in foreign affairs. This was because the monarch, as head of state, was the only person on the same level as the foreign rulers with which the foreign office had to conduct relations. Monarchs addressed each other as 'Cousin' in diplomatic and personal correspondence to signify their acceptance of an equality between them which did not apply to others and which denoted the idea that each sovereign ruler, great or otherwise, received his or her authority directly from God - i.e. by 'divine right'. For British foreign secretaries this meant that their work was conducted under two possible sources of interference. A great deal therefore depended on the strength of character and political strength of any individual foreign secretary. Some were able to take a fairly independent line - whilst others were appointed to act as directed by their prime minister. The extent to which a monarch was able to intervene in foreign affairs depended on the political situation, e.g. how strong the prime minister and/or foreign secretary were. Changing situations (a new monarch or prime minister or new political circumstances) could also affect the position of even a strong foreign secretary. The foreign secretary was (and is) accountable to Parliament for the foreign policy of the government. In the twentieth century we have become accustomed to the idea that governments are formed by a political party which controls the House of Commons - the House of Lords having declined in power to a mere shadow. In the first half of the nineteenth century governments, generally speaking, could not exercise this degree of control. They were frequently defeated over important issues of policy and often had to bow to the will of Parliament against their own preferred policy. This degree of accountability to an often unpredictable and independent Parliament represented another major constraint on foreign secretaries.

b) Transport and Communications

For most of the period 1815-65 the speed of communications between Britain and the outside world remained much as it had been during the eighteenth century. It was not until towards the end of this period that the availability of railways and the telegraph began to reduce the time between events occurring and their becoming known in London or between decisions being taken in London and their becoming known to British ambassadors based in other countries. In the 1830s dispatches between London and Paris took at least two days - depending on the time of the year and the weather they might take three days. Further afield, the time-delay between London and Madrid or St Petersburg varied from a minimum of ten days to over two weeks; whilst communications to and from Constantinople took around a month. Outside Europe (and relations between the European powers were not infrequently centred on events outside Europe), the waiting time was immense: three months for South America; sometimes as much as seven months for the Far East.

In such circumstances British foreign secretaries were highly dependent on the initiative, common sense and goodwill of their representatives on the spot. Only four of these British 'ministers' abroad held the top diplomatic rank of ambassador - those in France,

Austria, Russia and Turkey. Ambassadors or ministers who disagreed with their instructions had ample scope to follow their own policy and then justify this by claiming that events had changed the situation so much that their instructions were inoperable or irrelevant. Even those who were prepared to do as they were instructed often had to interpret their instructions in the light of events that could not have been foreseen at the time when the last Foreign Office despatch was drafted. These realities were recognised officially by the concession of extraordinary powers of discretion to some British representatives abroad: the High Commissioner in the Far East had the authority to declare war on China and ambassadors in Constantinople were occasionally given the power to summon the Royal Navy to support their diplomacy. Sometimes the Foreign Office had to by-pass the usual channels and give diplomatic powers to military or naval commanders operating far from home. Since even the passage of a day can sometimes see situations change dramatically, it was not surprising that foreign secretaries were frequently more at the mercy of events than in control of them.

c) Trade and Commerce

As has been noted above, foreign secretaries were highly accountable to Parliament. In the House of Commons, in particular, this meant to the interests of trade and commerce. By the early nineteenth century British politics were no longer so focused on the needs of agriculture - indeed they had never been completely dominated by agricultural concerns. The increasing size of the industrial sector further enhanced the long-established importance of exports and access to raw materials. Banking and commercial activities increased and more and more British capital investment took place outside Britain. Landowners, still by far the dominant group in the Commons, were increasingly diversifying into other areas - investing in canals, mining, factories and later railways. The commercial and trading interests expected it to be a prime function of British foreign policy to protect their trading interests, especially trade routes.

The Indian Empire was a significant and relatively new factor in Britain's imperial economy. Only brought substantially under British control in the second half of the eighteenth century, India was the source of many valuable commodities and a seemingly limitless market for British manufactures. The defence of routes to the Far East, and the security of India itself added a new dimension to Britain's relationship with the Turkish Empire, a trading partner since the sixteenth century and now a key strategic area for communications with India. In these and, indeed, in all areas of the globe where British merchants were pressing forward in search of new markets and new raw materials, the government was expected to be able to protect British interests - with diplomatic activity if possible - with force if necessary.

d) The Foreign Office

The Foreign Office was the most demanding of all the great political offices in the early nineteenth century. In other offices of state it was generally possible for the occupants to avoid unremitting hard work if so inclined. However, a foreign secretary could not escape for long from the enormous burden of day-to-day administration which went on all year round, even when Parliament was in recess.

Contrary to what might be supposed, a foreign secretary rarely left London - let alone travelled abroad. The circumstances which led to Lord Castlereagh spending significant periods on the continent in 1814 and 1815 were exceptional. His two best known successors, George Canning and Lord Palmerston, conducted affairs almost entirely from London using emissaries when necessary. All these men worked crippling schedules of 12 to 16 hours a day either at the Foreign Office itself or at their London homes. Palmerston (who had an ill-deserved reputation for laziness), even had a high table specially constructed so that he could work standing up when he became too tired to avoid nodding-off in a seated position!

The pressures at the Foreign Office were intensified by the erratic quality of the assistants on whom the hard-pressed minister was forced to rely. Clerks were appointed not so much for their ability as because of family and political connection. Some were hard-working; some were able. However, it was rare to find both virtues in the same individual, and many displayed neither quality. This left the minister with the task of trying to impose a degree of discipline on his clerks and having to do much of the basic work of drafting dispatches personally. An additional complication was that all incoming correspondence from foreign powers had to be translated from French (the standard language of diplomacy) into English and outward-bound dispatches had to be translated into French before transmission. Although most foreign secretaries, as well-educated men, had at least a reasonable command of French, in the period with which we are concerned only Palmerston had a sufficient degree of competence to be able to read and write French with total fluency at the high level required for diplomatic work. Ironically, it was Palmerston who reduced the work-burden of the Foreign Office in the 1830s by decreeing that dispatches would be sent in English in future, leaving the recipients to arrange for translation.

e) The Maintenance of Peace

Given the number of conflicts in which Britain had been involved in the eighteenth century (see pages 8-13) and given that in 1815 peace finally returned after twenty-two years of warfare in which there had been only one short cessation of hostilities between 1801 and 1803, it might seem odd to assert that the maintenance of peace was a most important objective of British foreign policy. Nevertheless, within the limits which the protection of British interests imposed, it can generally be said that Britain did genuinely seek to avoid war wherever, or for as long as, possible. In the most recent conflict against France, William Pitt, the great Prime Minister who had held office from 1783 to 1801 and again from 1804 to 1806, had initially done his best to avoid war. He had ignored the entreaties of the European sovereigns in 1790 to intervene to put down the French Revolution and had maintained that line even through the execution of the French King and Queen and the great terror which followed. What he could not ignore was the advance of the French revolutionary armies into Belgium in 1793. War against a revolutionary France could be avoided - war against an expansionist France (revolutionary or otherwise) could not. War is not, generally speaking, good for trade, though it may in the short term benefit certain sectors of the economy. Wars are expensive. To fight them governments need to raise money either by loans or by taxation - usually both. It was simply not in the interest of Britain, as a trading nation with high levels of private investment and relying on stability of supplies and markets, to become involved in wars unless there was some clear overriding necessity.

3 Britain and the Great Powers of Europe: Background to 1815

In this introductory chapter we need to review Britain's relationships with the other major European powers so as to provide some frame of reference for the events of the period 1815-65. Before looking in turn at each power, a general survey of Britain's eighteenth century diplomatic and strategic position would be useful. The Royal Navy exercised effective control of the Atlantic Ocean with that grip being especially tight in the North Atlantic. The Mediterranean was controlled by British possession of Gibraltar, ceded by Spain in 1713, and by the occupation of Menorca. Until the opening of the Suez Canal in 1869 Gibraltar controlled the only sea access to the Mediterranean and the Black Sea from the oceans of the world; Menorca provided a natural harbour where a British fleet could be based. Close ties were maintained with Portugal, the independence of which was seen as a major British interest. Portugal was important because it was en route to Gibraltar and gave direct access to the North Atlantic. Portugal also held the Madeira Islands which occupied an important strategic position in the Atlantic. Close ties were also maintained with the Netherlands which, until 1830, controlled the whole of the Low Countries.

One final point to consider is the implication of Britain's position as an island, detached from the European mainland. Fundamentally of course this was the basis of British security since it meant that Britain could not be directly attacked successfully unless an opponent first obtained command of the seas. This remained true even in the period of the Second World War, 1939-45, when air power had become a new and critical factor in warfare. On the other hand, Britain's island status also meant that it was difficult for Britain alone to come to grips with a continental enemy, superior in size and population and with supply lines stretching deep into Europe, away from the mighty hand of the Royal Navy. Britain, as Churchill noted above, traditionally worked in combination with other European powers. Churchill tended to present this as Britain coming to the aid of the oppressed and magnanimously delivering them from the tyrant of the day. Whatever the truth of this, it was certainly the case that continental allies were a necessity if war against a major European power was to be prosecuted successfully on the continent itself, rather than as a containing action based on control of the sea lanes. In other words, Britain could probably always defend herself against a single aggressor or even a couple of powers in combination, but actually to defeat the enemy allies were needed. Britain also had to guard against the possibility of a continental power uniting the whole of Europe against her because such an alliance of powers was the one thing which Britain might not be able to resist indefinitely. With these basic points in mind we can now proceed to analyse the relationships between Britain and the great powers.

a) France

France had been, since the later part of the seventeenth century, the strongest of all the continental powers. Paris was the centre of continental diplomacy and culture and French was the language of the educated aristocratic classes in all countries. Even as far away as Russia, the aristocracy habitually spoke French among themselves, using their native tongue only when dealing with their less-educated countrymen, or when it suited them to preserve confidentiality. Britain, interestingly enough, was an exception to this rule. In Britain the aristocratic classes spoke English and used French only when conversing with other nationalities. Nor was fluency in French by any means the rule. Many members of the aristocracy had only the barest grasp of the rudiments of French and total fluency was rare. The use of French amongst the British aristocracy had been declining since the fourteenth century and by the early nineteenth century it was a major source of annoyance to continental aristocrats that their British counterparts were so notoriously deficient in such a vital area of social intercourse.

During the eighteenth century Britain had engaged in a series of conflicts with France. At the beginning of the century in the so-called War of the Spanish Succession (1702-13), Britain had played a major part in a continental alliance against the power of the French King, Louis XIV. In the 1740s, during the confused conflicts known generally as the War of the Austrian Succession, Britain had fought against France and Spain. Then in 1756-63 had come the Seven Years' War in North America in which Britain had destroyed French power in Canada - this war is known (probably more meaningfully) to American historians as the Great War for the Empire. During the American War of Independence (1776-83), the French had sided with the American rebels and helped to secure the British acceptance of American independence. Finally, in 1793 Britain had declared war on France, thus beginning a conflict which ended with the defeat of the French Empire of Napoleon Bonaparte in 1815. In all these conflicts Britain had worked in concert with European allies. The defeat of the Napoleonic Empire which had effectively encompassed the whole of the Western half of the continent had been achieved by a Grand Alliance of Britain and the other European powers (see pages 18-19).

With such a history it was inevitable that Anglo-French rivalry and tension had become a deeply embedded part of the general diplomatic scene in Europe. The complete defeat of Bonaparte in 1814-15 opened up an opportunity for Britain to put an end to this situation of almost continuous hostility. Bonaparte had swept away many of the old boundaries and rulers of Europe - in effect he had remade Europe in a form suited to the continued dominance of France. Britain now had an opportunity, in concert with her allies, to dismantle that system and construct a new order in which security against France would be a guiding factor. At the same time, Britain could play the role of an intermediary, protecting France from the most penal demands of those European powers which had suffered humiliation at French hands over the previous two decades. In this way it was hoped that Anglo-French relations could be placed on a better footing. Nor was this desire for better relations entirely new. In the early days of the French Revolution William Pitt had expressed the hope that the end of absolutism in France and the emergence of a constitutional monarchy might usher in a new era of harmony between the two countries. In the event, as the following chapters will demonstrate, Anglo-French relations did not much improve after 1815. However, the other objective of securing Europe against future French expansionism was achieved. It should also be noted that although Anglo-French relations were often bad during the rest of the nineteenth century, and war between the two countries often seemed close, no actual wars occurred and in 1854-6 there was even an alliance between them against Russia in the Crimean War.

b) Russia

In the first half of the eighteenth century Britain had taken hardly any notice of Russia at all. However, in the later years of the century this had begun to change because of the active foreign policy of the

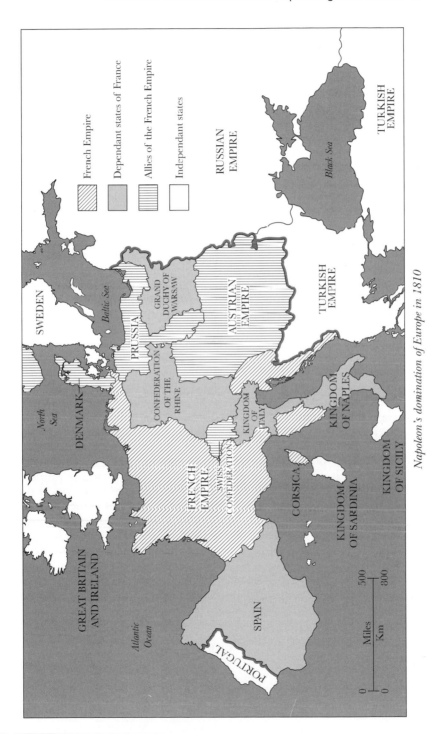

French Empire

Dependant states of France

Allies of the French Empire

Independant states

RUSSIAN EMPIRE

TURKISH EMPIRE

TURKISH EMPIRE

Black Sea

SWEDEN

Baltic Sea

PRUSSIA

GRAND DUCHY OF WARSAW

AUSTRIAN EMPIRE

TURKISH EMPIRE

CONFEDERATION OF THE RHINE

North Sea

DENMARK

KINGDOM OF ITALY

KINGDOM OF NAPLES

FRENCH EMPIRE

SWISS CONFEDERATION

CORSICA

KINGDOM OF SICILY

GREAT BRITAIN AND IRELAND

KINGDOM OF SARDINIA

Atlantic Ocean

SPAIN

PORTUGAL

Miles

Km

0   500

0   300

Napoleon's domination of Europe in 1810

Russian Empress, Catherine the Great, who ruled from 1762 to 1796. Under Catherine the Russian Empire had expanded considerably: south to the Black Sea through wars with Turkey in 1774 and 1792 and west through a series of partitions of Poland in 1772, 1793 and 1795. These developments attracted relatively little British attention as they did not seem for the moment to threaten any vital British interests. One factor in Anglo-Russian relations which started to emerge during this period was that of India. Russia was an Asiatic power as well as a European one and the possibility of a conflict of interests was inherent in the development of Britain's Indian Empire. However, William Pitt saw the rise of Russia as primarily a factor influencing the balance of power in Europe favourably. Here was a possible counter to French power which, properly managed, might help to promote greater stability on the continent. Russia was a crucial element in the defeat of Napoleon and in the system of security against France. A sound relationship with Russia therefore became, and was to remain, a central aim of British foreign policy, though it was not always possible to maintain harmony in the years after 1815. The great figures in British foreign policy of the first half of the nineteenth century, Castlereagh, Canning, Palmerston and Aberdeen, all strove to follow, in their own ways, the policy of Pitt - harmony and cooperation with Russia - despite the fact that it was not always an easy path.

c) The Austrian (or Habsburg) Empire

Austria was important to Britain in the eighteenth century because, although clearly inferior in power to France, it was the most credible alternative leading nation and therefore the most important potential British ally. The problem with Austria was that not only was it weaker than France, it was also a declining power. The Austrian Empire covered a great variety of nationalities, and because there was little common feeling between them there was a general reluctance to cooperate with one another. Nevertheless Austria's strategic position in the centre of Europe ensured that it would be important as long as the Empire survived (it did not collapse in the end until the First World War), and therefore, like Russia, Austria was part of the key to defeating and subsequently controlling France. Palmerston summed up the position in the 1840s when he observed:

1 Austria is a most important element in the balance of European power, a barrier against encroachment on the one side, and against invasion on the other. The political independence and liberties of Europe are bound up with the maintenance and integrity of Austria as a great European
5 power; and therefore anything which weakens Austria must be something which Englishmen ought to try to prevent.

In referring to Austria as a two-way barrier, Palmerston had in mind the problem which had existed since the conclusion of the Napoleonic Wars, that of not allowing Russia to become too strong in its role as a guardian against France. Lying between these two potentially dominating forces, Austria was in a crucial position. Its weakness in serving this purpose was recognised by Britain's acceptance of the emerging power of Prussia after 1815.

d) Prussia

Prussia had been founded as a kingdom in its own right as recently as 1701. Two great kings, Frederick William (1713-40) and Frederick II also known as 'Frederick the Great' (1740-86) were responsible for consolidating and expanding Prussia in the eighteenth century, but at the time of the Napoleonic Wars Prussia did not formally rank as a great power in Europe. Nevertheless Frederick II had turned Prussia into a strong military state and by the time of his death Prussia had already achieved a measure of acceptance as a rising power by joining in the first partition of Poland with Russia and Austria in 1772. From the British point of view the rise of Prussia meant that there was another viable force on the continent which might provide a possible ally in war or counterbalance in diplomacy. Certainly William Pitt, the Prime Minister at the time of the French Revolution and the subsequent French Wars, believed that Prussia could be a valuable asset as part of a general coalition against the French. However, the Prussian King, Frederick William III (1797-1849), pursued a neutral policy in response to the initial conquests of Napoleon Bonaparte and when he did at last declare war on France in 1806 he was decisively defeated at the battles of Jena and Auerstadt with a resulting heavy loss of territory. Following this Prussia underwent a great deal of internal military reorganisation and emerged alongside Russia to share in the decisive victory over Bonaparte at Leipzig in 1813. It was Prussian troops which joined with the British forces to secure the final defeat of Bonaparte at Waterloo in June 1815, but even before that Britain had clearly recognised Prussia as a crucial element in the future diplomacy of Europe in the preliminary agreements which would lead to the Vienna Settlement of 1815.

4 1815-65: An Overview

The period which this book covers was very largely a peaceful one for Britain and Europe. The one major exception to this was the Crimean War of 1854-6 (see Chapter 5) in which Britain joined with France to defeat Russia. The period from the British point of view is marked largely by the desire to prevent hostilities recurring on any general basis after 1815. The long periods of war between 1793 and 1815 had put an enormous strain on the Treasury and there was a general reluctance at government level to undergo such financial trauma again. British policy towards Europe in this period was thus conditioned by a strong inclination to try to preserve the Vienna Settlement by which the Revolutionary and Napoleonic Wars were brought to an end in 1815 (see next chapter). If at times it could not be preserved to the letter, then Britain strove to ensure that, so far as possible, the spirit of the Settlement was maintained. In general terms, this period saw Britain attempting to maintain the peace and stability of Europe, acting in a kind of arbitrative and monitorial role made credible by the prestige gained from having stood out so long alone against Bonaparte and then having contributed significantly to his downfall. However, within this framework, there was a gradual change in the general view in Britain of the two main powers, France and Russia. Whilst Britain kept a close eye on the ambitions of both there was no doubt that in 1815 Britain's main priority was to guard against France and that Russia was potentially its most effective ally in achieving this. By 1865 this situation had in effect been reversed. Russia, defeated in 1856 in the Crimea, had been subjected to a stringent peace aimed at curtailing its ambitions, and France was seen as the principal British ally in maintaining that security.

Making notes on 'Introduction: British Foreign Policy - Principles and Practice'

This chapter has introduced you to two ideas which you need to carry forward in your work on the rest of this book. The first is that there were certain vital interests at stake for Britain in relation to the balance of power in Europe and that protecting these interests had come to be identified with preventing the domination of Europe by any one power. The second is that Britain had no fixed allegiances in Europe but relied upon rallying and coordinating resistance to a dominant power as the need arose. Short notes which you can refer to easily to hold a focus on these points will be of use as you consider the issues and events which were important from 1815 onwards.

1. What were the strategic implications of Britain's position in relation to Continental Europe?
2. What economic interests did Britain have to safeguard in 1815? How were these affected by European issues?
3. What were the key issues in maintaining a balance of power in Europe?
a) summarise very briefly Britain's attitude to each of the major powers, and
b) consider the practical difficulties Britain faced in dealing with European affairs.
4. What were the implications of Britain's status as a 'constitutional monarchy'?

2 Britain and the European Settlement - 1815

1 Introduction: The Background to Castlereagh's Policy

a) Lord Castlereagh

Castlereagh's background was the Ulster gentry. Although his mother came from the English aristocracy, he cannot really be seen as coming from a long line of aristocrats. His father, the Marquess of Londonderry, had been raised to the Irish peerage in his own lifetime and his title did not carry the right of entry to the House of Lords - this being restricted to a limited number of Irish peers under the Act of Union of 1800. Castlereagh was therefore an MP throughout his career. He had entered politics as a disciple of the great Prime Minister, William Pitt (1783-1801 and 1804-06). After the death of Pitt in 1806 he continued to serve under successive prime ministers until 1809, when he had a serious row when his Cabinet colleague, George Canning, which resulted in the two men fighting a duel in which Canning received a minor bullet wound. After this they both resigned and Castlereagh did not return to office until February 1812 when he accepted the post of Foreign Secretary under Spencer Percival. In May 1812 Percival was assassinated by a lunatic who shot him dead in the lobby of the House of Commons. After a short period of political confusion, Lord Liverpool emerged as the most acceptable replacement as Prime Minister. Since Liverpool was in the House of Lords, Castlereagh became extremely important to the new government as the leading man in the House of Commons. This was made even more the case due to Canning's refusal to join the government other than on totally unacceptable terms. Castlereagh was thus compelled to take on the job of Leader of the House of Commons as well as remaining Foreign Secretary - a tremendous burden of work, which may well have been a factor in his mental breakdown and suicide in 1822.

b) The Problems Facing Castlereagh in 1812

Castlereagh's foreign policy in 1812 was dictated by the war and the need to end it successfully and quickly. Successfully, from the British point of view, meant that the size of the French Empire must be drastically reduced so that the country was not much larger than it had been before the Revolution broke out in 1789. Furthermore it meant that a security system had to be put in place which would prevent any further French expansion in the future. Finally, it meant that whatever arrangements were made should not set up further causes of conflicts which might lead to a general war or place some other continental power in such a dominant position that it might replace France as a threat to British security. 1812 was a crucial year in that it was the year in which the war turned decisively against Napoleon Bonaparte. First, he lost control of the Spanish Peninsula; second, his ill-fated attempt to invade Russia cost him massive casualties and loss of prestige, and left him vulnerable to a concerted effort by the other major powers. Even so, for many months up to the final defeat of France, Castlereagh and other European statesmen tended to assume that the problem facing them was to force Bonaparte to accept terms which would ensure future peace. Only slowly did it become clear that his complete overthrow would be the only solution offering a guarantee that France would not attempt to expand its territory almost immediately.

In addition, it was imperative from the British point of view that peace be achieved as quickly as possible. Why was this? There were two fundamental reasons. The first was financial and economic. By 1812 Britain had been at war almost continuously since 1793. This had been an enormous burden on the Treasury and vast amounts of money had had to be raised in taxation and even more in loans to pay for the war effort. As well as maintaining both a naval blockade against France and increasingly large armies in Europe, Britain had also had to take on the responsibility for financing allies in a series of coalitions. In 1793 the British National Debt (the total amount owed by the government to its creditors) had stood at £234 million and had been falling from this figure, considered high at the time, under the careful budgeting of William Pitt. By 1815, when the war finally ended, the National Debt stood at £834 million and paying the interest on this was a huge burden on the public finances. To make matters worse, economic warfare with France imposed by Bonaparte's 'continental system' had disrupted trade which was the basis of Britain's wealth and prosperity. A return to peace was therefore crucial to the economy and government finance. In simple terms, the country could not afford to carry on the war much longer.

The financial and economic pressures on Britain to end the European War were reinforced by social and political pressures, the second fundamental reason. The impact of the war on the economy produced social discontent. Agricultural prices rose steeply as government orders for cereals, livestock and wool to support the war effort pushed up demand to unprecedented heights. This was good news for landowners and tenant farmers who saw their profits rising, but it was bad news for the rest of the population which found bread prices rising, sometimes beyond their capacity to pay. With the population rapidly increasing at the same time, farmers found no shortage of labour available for their extra production and it did not prove necessary to raise the level of agricultural wages. In industry some workers benefited from rising wages but many others found demand for their labour falling or their skills being overtaken by the march of technology. Social discontent increased the government's awareness of the impact of the political ideas of the French Revolution, which stressed liberty and the equality of social classes. By 1800 the government had introduced tough new laws to curb the activities of radicals and trade unions (or 'combinations' of workmen) were outlawed. However, these laws were far from effective. Trade unions continued to exist and even increase in numbers and membership. In 1812 the assassination of the Prime Minister, Spencer Percival, was celebrated with riotous street parties in towns up and down the country. The government was appalled and feared a general insurrection. Though subsequent investigations failed to reveal any revolutionary plots, the fear that the population was on the verge of revolt constituted another powerful argument for ending the war and returning things to normal as soon as possible.

2 The Defeat of France

a) The Formation of the Fourth Coalition Against France

To defeat Napoleon required the combined efforts of the European powers and Castlereagh's first priority was to construct a coalition capable of exploiting the opportunities created by the events of 1812. Fortunately Bonaparte had done much of the groundwork himself. His abortive invasion of Russia in 1812 convinced Tsar Alexander I to issue a proclamation in February 1813 in which he pledged himself to bring 'peace and independence to nations prepared to face sacrifices to achieve this end'. Shortly afterwards the Russians concluded an alliance with Prussia. Initially this alliance was unsuccessful in its attempts to carry the war forward against Bonaparte. However, the French were too weak to follow up their successes. The collaboration between Russia and Prussia thoroughly alarmed the Austrian Chancellor, Prince Metternich, who had no wish to see French hegemony in Europe replaced by that of Russia and who also feared that Prussia might displace Austria as the dominant German presence in central Europe. Metternich therefore sponsored an armistice with Bonaparte and secured peace proposals acceptable to the Tsar which were put forward as the Treaty of Reichenbach in June 1813. This would have left France with its borders on the Rhine and the Alps and with parts of Italy and Spain still under its control. It would have meant that she retained some of its territorial gains. Metternich cemented this deal with the Russians and Prussians by agreeing that if Bonaparte would not accept this offer, Austria would join the alliance. Whether Austria would have honoured this commitment if the situation had remained unchanged is debatable, but shortly before the armistice was due to run out, Wellington won a great victory over French forces in

Spain at the battle of Vittoria. This stiffened the Austrian resolve and they joined the war against France in August after Bonaparte had failed to accept the terms offered. In October 1813 the Bavarians broke with Bonaparte and joined the alliance. Since Sweden had already been won over to the British side in March by the promise that Norway (then Danish-owned) could be annexed, the coalition of powers against France was now formidable. All that was required was a guarantee of funding from Britain which was duly offered.

b) Castlereagh's Policy 1812-13

As can be seen from the previous section, Castlereagh was largely a spectator during the diplomatic developments of 1812 and 1813. Officially, British policy was to secure the complete defeat of Bonaparte and his expulsion from European affairs. However, privately Castlereagh was only too aware that this might not be possible or even sensible. He knew that Britain could not force the European powers to fight France if they chose to make a deal. He also knew that Britain could not inflict a final defeat on France alone. Additionally he knew that the alternative to Bonaparte continuing in power in France was most likely to be the restoration of the Bourbon monarchy - regarded by the British government as distinguished only by its crass stupidity. Castlereagh had to accept that the eventual peace settlement might involve Bonaparte remaining in control of France but he feared that such a settlement might prove short-lived since in his judgement the French Emperor would always be a threat. In the meantime, his only direct achievement was the securing of the agreement with Sweden, a move which was not popular in Parliament where sympathy for Norway was strong. Late in 1812 he had tried an appeal to the Austrians to enter an alliance but Metternich, who had seen Austria crushed too often by Bonaparte in the past, was not to be tempted at that stage. The process by which the Russians brought the Prussians into the war against France was welcome, but Metternich's initiative in securing an armistice was greeted by Castlereagh with dismay. In September he tried to stiffen allied resolve with a proposal for a Grand Alliance, in which all the existing agreements between the various allies would be replaced with one comprehensive alliance. He summed up his thinking in a despatch to his Ambassador to Russia in September 1813:

1   The Sovereigns of ... Europe have at last confederated for their common safety, having in vain sought that safety in detached and insulated compromises with the enemy. They have successively found that no extent of submission could procure for them either safety or repose,
5   and that they no sooner ceased to be objects of hostility themselves, than they were compelled to become instruments in the hands of France for ... the conquest of other unoffending states ... a peace con-

cluded in concert, though less advantageous in its terms, would be
preferable to the largest concessions received from their enemy as the
10 price of disunion. The great object of the Allies, whether in war or
negotiation, should be to keep together, and to drive back and confine
the armies of France ... It is by the war in Spain that Russia has been
preserved, and that Germany may be delivered; it is by the war in
15 Germany that Spain may look to escape ... subjugation ... To determine to stand or fall together is their only safety, and to effect this the
confederates must be brought to agree to certain fixed principles of
common interest ...

The European powers, and especially Metternich, kept this idea at
arm's length for the time being. Castlereagh, increasingly frustrated,
complained that Metternich treated the war, not as a 'contest of
nations' but as 'a game of statesmen'; a matter for negotiations and
diplomatic strategy rather than hard fighting. However, the issues of
peace or war were effectively out of Castlereagh's hands for the rest of
1813 as Metternich took centre stage. It was Bonaparte's obstinacy
which had brought Austria into the war and even after this
Metternich did not give up his efforts to reach an accommodation
with the French Emperor. In time, however, the principles advocated
by Castlereagh came increasingly to the fore.

c) The Tide Turns Against Bonaparte

In mid-October 1813 Bonaparte suffered a crucial defeat at Leipzig.
As a result, the members of the Confederation of the Rhine deserted
France and joined the coalition. Metternich saw this as a new oppor-
tunity to bring Bonaparte to terms and devised the so-called
'Frankfurt Proposals' in November under which France would still
have occupied its 'natural frontiers' with borders on the Pyrenees, the
Alps and the Rhine. The news of this offer appalled Castlereagh who
saw how unpopular it would be in Britain. He immediately
despatched protests to the European allies arguing that so large a
France would be dangerous and that Bonaparte could not be trusted.
Nevertheless, he was forced to admit that if the deal went through
Britain would be powerless to prevent it. Once again Bonaparte
himself came to Castlereagh's aid. He delayed acceptance of the
Frankfurt Proposals in the hope that the fortunes of war would swing
his way and enable him to secure better terms. By the time he finally
made up his mind to accept them the terms themselves had been
overtaken by events.

At the end of 1813 the British government agreed that Castlereagh
should go to the continent to conduct the diplomatic negotiations
with Britain's allies and the French personally. Castlereagh reached
Basle in mid-January 1813 and there met with Metternich. It was a
meeting which was to prove decisive to the course of European diplo-

macy for the next few years. The two men, who had hitherto disliked and distrusted each other's policies, found, through personal contact, an unexpected degree of mutual trust and understanding. Castlereagh agreed that attempts to find a compromise with Bonaparte should proceed - he was increasingly confident that these would fail anyway. Metternich agreed that in the long run the future peace of Europe would be best served if the choice between Bonaparte and the Bourbons was left to the French people. Meanwhile French resistance was faltering. Wellington had entered France across the Pyrenees and allied forces crossed the Rhine. At the end of March the allies entered Paris itself and on 6 April 1814 Bonaparte agreed to an unconditional abdication.

3 Making the Peace - 1814

Even before the entry of allied troops into Paris, Castlereagh had taken the initiative on the diplomatic front. With French resistance crumbling away he urged the need once more for a comprehensive agreement which would ensure that the allies remained united. This time the allies were receptive to his ideas and the result was the Treaty of Chaumont of March 1814 by which Austria, Prussia, Russia and Britain agreed to join for a period of twenty years after any peace settlement to defend the arrangements made. Many of the eventual decisions of the Congress of Vienna were formulated at this point:

(i) An enlarged and independent Holland to act as a secure buffer against France.
(ii) A confederation of the German states.
(iii) An independent Switzerland.
(iv) A Bourbon restoration in Spain.
(v) The restoration of the Italian states.

The issue of what was to be done about the government of France was left open - the increasing assumption being that the French themselves would ultimately decide. In the end, the matter was resolved in the immediate aftermath of the allied entry into Paris. The veteran French politician and diplomat, Talleyrand who had survived the Revolution and served Bonaparte for a time, persuaded the Tsar that a Bourbon restoration was both essential for the future stability of Europe and in accordance with the wishes of the French people. To reinforce his case he used the argument that the Bourbons had a 'legitimate' right to the throne of France. A provisional government was organised by Talleyrand which then deposed Bonaparte who, faced with the collapse of both his military and political support, had no real alternative other than to abdicate.

Castlereagh was willing to accept the return of the Bourbons despite his misgivings about their capacities as rulers. His main preoccupation now was that the peace imposed on France should be balanced, workable and in accordance with British interests. What did this mean in practice? It certainly meant that there should be a system of security which would curtail any further French expansionism. On the other hand, Castlereagh was well aware that a settlement which was too penal would have the effect of leaving France resentful and determined to reverse the settlement, or at least parts of it, possibly by force. Such a settlement could not be in British interests and Castlereagh knew that the one thing his colleagues in London expected of him above all was that there should be a long, effectively permanent, peace during which Britain could recover from the financial and economic strains which had been endured for over twenty years.

Castlereagh believed that he had secured his aims in the terms of the Peace of Paris which was agreed with the restored Bourbon King, Louis XVIII, on 30 May 1814. Under this agreement France was required to pay no compensation to any other country for the wars and the eastern border of France still included parts of both Germany and Belgium. France was required to surrender some Caribbean territories to Britain but overall it was a very moderate set of terms which Castlereagh hoped would have the effect of strengthening the position of the new King. Bonaparte was also treated relatively leniently in a separate agreement concluded shortly after his abdication. In this he was granted the island of Elba in full sovereignty along with an income of 2 million francs a year from France - the condition being that he remain permanently in exile on Elba, which, situated in the northern Mediterranean between Corsica and the Italian mainland, was, perhaps, unwisely close to France.

4 The Congress of Vienna

a) The Purpose of the Congress

Although Bonaparte had been defeated and exiled and a peace concluded with France, there remained a great deal of work to be done before Europe could be considered safe and stable for the future. The impact of the French Empire had been so great that the map of Europe had virtually been redrawn over the previous twenty years. Rulers had been overthrown and new states brought into being, as Tolstoy's character, Countess Rostov, observes in *War and Peace* - 'after Napoleon nothing will ever be the same again'. The question of to what extent there should be an attempt to restore things to the way they had been on the eve of the French Revolution was precisely what was occupying the minds of Castlereagh and the other allied leaders. The idea behind a grand congress was to try to give at least the impression that all nations would be party to the decisions taken over the resettlement of Europe. To this end the allies decided to invite virtually every European state to attend the conferences in Vienna.

For six months prior to the meeting Britain, Prussia, Russia and Austria discussed the final terms of the peace. They were determined to keep all the major issues and decisions under their immediate control and as a result many important points were actually settled even before the Congress met in October 1814.

b) Castlereagh's Policy at Vienna

Castlereagh based his policy on Pitt's original plans dating back to 1804, with the drafting of which he had personally assisted the great man. Pitt had planned that Prussia should expand in the north and west of Germany while Austria would expand its territory and influence in Italy. This was intended to act both as a barrier to France but also to compensate for the increased power and influence of Russia which Pitt correctly calculated was bound to move further westwards into Europe. Pitt also envisaged that Belgium should be combined with Holland to provide a more secure buffer state to prevent France expanding in future into the Low Countries - a particular requirement for British interests.

Castlereagh was also influenced by Pitt's plans for the longer-term security of Europe. According to Pitt it was not enough simply to agree upon the terms of the settlement. Once the settlement was in place it would need to be protected. In a communication to the Russians in January 1805 Pitt had set out his views on how this might be achieved:

I   Supposing the efforts of the Allies to have been completely successful [i.e. in winning the war], His Majesty would nevertheless consider this salutary work as still imperfect, if the restoration of peace were not accompanied by the most effectual measures for giving solidity and per-
5   manence to the system which shall thus have been established. Much will undoubtedly be effected for the future repose of Europe by these territorial arrangements, which will furnish a more effectual barrier than has before existed against the ambition of France. But in order to render this security as complete as possible, it seems necessary, at the
10   period of a general pacification, to form a treaty to which all the principal powers of Europe should be parties, by which their respective rights and possessions, as they then have been established, shall be fixed and recognized, and they should bind themselves mutually to protect and support each other, against any attempt to infringe them - It [i.e. the
15   treaty] should re-establish a general and comprehensive system of public law in Europe, and provide, as far as possible, for repressing future attempts to disturb the general tranquillity, and above all, for restraining any projects of aggrandizement and ambition similar to those which have produced all the calamities inflicted on Europe since the disastrous
20   era of the French Revolution. This treaty should be put under the special guarantee of Great Britain and Russia, and the two powers should, by a

separate engagement, bind themselves to each other jointly to take an active part in preventing its being infringed ...

By the time of the Congress of Vienna the situation had changed to the extent that Castlereagh was almost as concerned about the problem that Russian power might pose in the future as he was about the possible resurgence of France. Pitt's reference to a special relationship with Russia reflected the fact that at that point in time it was the Russians who had made the first move to seek an alliance against France. Castlereagh was now inclined to disregard this idea because he feared that the Tsar might use such an arrangement as a pretext to intervene whenever he chose in the affairs of other countries. The Tsar was an extremely unpredictable man who veered between apparent liberality and generosity of spirit, and autocratic authoritarianism. Castlereagh believed that cooperation and understanding with Metternich now offered the best hope for maintaining stability in Europe and managing the Tsar. However, the rest of Pitt's concept for a 'Concert of Europe', in which the powers would collaborate to maintain peace and their mutual interests, still remained at the heart of his policy. In May 1815 he used extracts from Pitt's Memorandum in the House of Commons to justify the policy he was pursuing and silence critics who were still influenced by the reputation of the great Pitt even a decade after his death.

c) The Terms of the Settlement

i) Great Britain
Britain naturally had no interest in territorial gains other than outside of mainland Europe. Under the Treaty of Chaumont Britain was already entitled to gains at French expense in the Caribbean. However, Castlereagh was under pressure from commercial interests to increase the security of trade routes. To this end and for general strategic purposes Britain also secured Heligoland in the North Sea and Cape Colony in South Africa, both from the Dutch; Malta and the Ionian Islands in the Mediterranean which, together with Gibraltar, ensured virtual British control of that Sea; and Ceylon (modern Sri Lanka) was taken under British control to further strengthen the security of the Indian Empire.

ii) Russia
The Tsar had expansionist ambitions which could not be entirely resisted, although Castlereagh was prepared to place some limitations on them even at the cost of war if the Russians proved unwilling to compromise. He was prepared to accept that some extension of Russian influence would be legitimate and beneficial to the security of Europe, although, of course, he was not prepared to allow this to go

the length of setting up Russia as the final arbiter of Europe. Given the parlous state of British finances in 1815, the fact that Castlereagh could contemplate a renewal of hostilities with Russia is testimony to how seriously this potential threat was taken. In the end Russia gained Finland which had already been taken from Sweden during the course of the war, and Bessarabia which had been taken from Turkey. In effect, there was little that the other powers, including Britain, could have done about either of these annexations even if they had been so inclined. The real problem was over Poland - it was this that brought the powers close to a complete breakdown in relations. In the late eighteenth century Poland had been subjected to three partitions (1772, 1793 and 1795) as a result of which it had ceased to exist as an independent state. Polish territory had been divided between Russia, Prussia and Austria. Bonaparte's conquest of central and eastern Europe had overthrown this arrangement. He had set up a Polish state (the Grand Duchy of Warsaw) as part of the French Empire's dependent territory (see the map on page 11). The Tsar now wanted to incorporate the whole of Poland into the Russian Empire as a separately-ruled kingdom with himself as King. He aimed to compensate the Prussians with Saxony.

Castlereagh was opposed to this solution of the Polish Question and in this he was supported by Metternich. Both feared that the Tsar was going to turn into another Bonaparte. Castlereagh came under great pressure from his Cabinet colleagues to give in over Poland. Liverpool was under great pressure in Parliament to reduce government spending and taxation and doubted whether Poland constituted a major British interest. However, Castlereagh was not shaken from his views. He insisted that the Tsar must be forced to accept some degree of compromise. Failure to do this, he argued, would lead to trouble between Prussia and Austria, since both could not be adequately compensated, and would give the Tsar the impression that he could do whatever he liked. In the end a compromise was reached, but only after hard words had been exchanged all round and military preparations had been put in hand (see page 33). Russia obtained the major portion of Poland with both Austria and Prussia changing their pre-war borders to provide the additional Polish territory. The Prussians were bought off with part of Saxony and the Austrians had at least retained some Polish territory as well as making Italian gains (see page 108).

iii) Prussia

The Prussians gained some two-fifths of Saxony and also retained part of Poland. The other major extension of Prussian power was achieved by the consolidation of a host of minute states in the Rhineland into a single block under Prussian control - this being justified as creating a barrier against the French as well as serving as compensation for denying Prussia the whole of Saxony.

iv) Austria
Castlereagh was particularly concerned to safeguard the influence and strategic viability of Austria, since he now saw it as the centrepiece of stability in central Europe. Austria had lost out in Germany to Prussia, for example in the Rhineland where Metternich's family had originated, and would also lose Belgium. The main compensation for this came in the form of Italian gains. Lombardy and Venetia were transferred to the Austrian Empire along with Salzburg and the Tyrol. Furthermore, the whole of Italy was recognised as an Austrian sphere of influence. Finally, Austria was given the leading role in the German Confederation which ensured that, in practice, it retained effective control in German affairs.

v) The Netherlands
Holland (the Netherlands) absorbed Belgium in order to strengthen its position against France and to compensate the Dutch, who had changed sides during the war, for losses to Britain. Luxembourg was also incorporated into the new Dutch state and given a Prussian garrison. For Castlereagh the security of the Low Countries, strategically important as a possible base for invasion of Britain and a major economic point of access for trade into Europe, was, of course, of major importance.

vi) The German states
There was no attempt to revive the old Holy Roman Empire which Bonaparte had swept away in 1806. Instead the European powers decided to simplify the pre-Napoleonic system in Germany by drastically reducing the number of states there from over 300 to 39 in a new German Confederation, the borders of which were drawn so as to include an amount of Prussian and Austrian territory.

vii) The Italian states
Piedmont was strengthened by being given Nice and Genoa. This made it a more effective barrier in north-west Italy against France. Elsewhere the principle of legitimacy was applied for the most part with the restoration of the original rulers, including His Holiness the Pope. However, a major exception was made in the case of Murat, the Bonapartist King of Naples who was initially allowed to keep his throne. This had been agreed under pressure from Austria in the winter of 1813-14 in order to keep Murat neutral in the coming struggle with Bonaparte. Castlereagh was against this but bowed to the wider arguments. In fact, the allies were considering whether to keep their agreement with Murat at the time when he decided to support Bonaparte's attempt to regain power in France in 1815. Grateful to have their dilemma resolved for them, the allies duly captured Murat, shot him and restored the Bourbon King, Ferdinand, to the throne.

d) The Principles Governing the Settlement

The fundamental principle which motivated the powers at Vienna was the need to secure themselves against further French aggression. As has already been seen, Castlereagh saw this as involving a balanced settlement which, while curtailing French power, would nevertheless leave the French with no grievances so pressing that they would be thirsting for revenge. This principle involved wider considerations. The great powers who had contributed most to the defeat of France were determined to strengthen their own positions or at least protect themselves as well as possible. They were only too aware that in doing this they might come into conflict with each other. To reduce the risk of this happening they therefore adopted the principle that wherever one great power agreed to defer to another it should be compensated elsewhere at the expense of weaker powers. This might in retrospect seem unfair and arbitrary, but at the time it seemed justifiable to the great powers in that they were attempting to safeguard the peace and stability of Europe. Their view was that, in order to achieve this, the smaller powers should be prepared to make sacrifices, which, in any case, would probably benefit them in the long run.

Another principle which was firmly in mind in the considerations described above was the need to preserve what was termed the 'balance of power'. Castlereagh and Metternich were agreed that the preservation of peace was dependent on the creation of what Castlereagh liked to call a 'just equilibrium' between the states of Europe in terms of their territory, population and resources. To this extent Castlereagh and Metternich were less concerned with increasing the power of their own countries than with limiting the power of others - as evidenced by their attitude to the Polish Question. Castlereagh clearly saw that this principle had to apply in reverse where France was concerned. He saw a danger that if France were weakened too much the overall balance of power would be adversely affected in that Russia would correspondingly become too strong. For this same reason he also recognised the need to bring Turkey into the general system of European security as a Russian neighbour and a power in south-eastern Europe (see page 88).

Legitimacy, as advocated by Talleyrand in the case of France, also became a principle of the settlement, although it was not applied automatically or consistently. As a principle, however, it was difficult to define. Talleyrand himself had no principles at all when it came to diplomacy and his use of the argument was based on a cynical calculation of French (and his own) interests. Castlereagh was inclined to take it more seriously, but for him it raised the difficult problem that restoring 'legitimate' monarchs in Europe generally meant restoring autocratic rulers and this was unpopular in Britain with its parliamentary traditions and constitutional monarchy. Metternich was much attracted to the principle of legitimacy - to him it seemed the way to bolster up the power of monarchy and aristocracy which he saw as the basis of European civilisation. However, he defined the concept as meaning that nations in effect had no right to exist without their legitimate ruler whose rights were sacrosanct. This idea was to cause problems between Castlereagh and Metternich in the years after Vienna. In any case, the principle of legitimacy, however defined, ultimately took second place to pragmatic considerations. If its application ran counter to the need to provide safeguards against France, or counter to the rewards envisaged for themselves by the victorious powers, it was disregarded.

e) The Return of Bonaparte

On 1 March 1815 Bonaparte landed at Cannes, in southern France, after escaping from Elba. He had less than a thousand armed men with him, but within three weeks he was in Paris and Louis XVIII had fled ignominiously to Ghent (in the Netherlands). Bonaparte's success was the result of a combination of factors. First, there was the residual appeal of his fame. The French people had accepted back the Bourbon monarchy without enthusiasm and the feeble Louis could not match Bonaparte's allure and the thought that even now he might restore French pride and glory. Secondly, he was a master of deception and strategy. Weak initially, he convinced the first troops sent to capture him that he was returning at the summons of the allies to Paris. He followed up this improbable claim by emotional appeals to the next contingents which closed in on his forces. So powerful was his personality that every force sent against him ended up joining him!

The allies in Vienna were stunned. Britain was forced to abandon plans for the demobilisation of armies and Parliament had to vote new taxation proposals through in order to provide funds to renew hostilities. Bonaparte knew of the difficulties the allies had encountered in the peace talks and hoped to exploit their divisions. He offered peace to Britain and Austria, calculating that these two powers were the most likely to respond and that without them he could deal with the rest. This ploy failed. The allies rallied around the terms of the Treaty of Chaumont and prepared to meet the challenge. It was to be a severe test. The Russian armies had already withdrawn to Poland and the Austrians were fully occupied by Murat who had mobilised his forces in support of Bonaparte. This left only the British and Prussian armies of the great powers immediately available, supported by the Dutch, Belgians and odd German contingents. In June, his diplomatic offensive having failed, Bonaparte advanced into Belgium and defeated the Prussians. However, his supporting force commanded by Marshal Ney was defeated by Dutch forces and on 18 June Wellington, with an army of British, Dutch, Belgians and Germans held Bonaparte's forces at Waterloo near Brussels. It was a turning point in

European history. In the evening, Prussian troops arrived at the French rear and Bonaparte was finished. Failing to escape to America, he surrendered to the British, who exiled him this time to St Helena in the far reaches of the South Atlantic where he died in 1821.

The effects of Bonaparte's last adventure threatened Castlereagh's achievement of the previous May. The lenient peace with France which he had done so much to sponsor now stood under review. The Prussians demanded new territorial gains from France, including Alsace and Lorraine, and also wanted heavy financial compensation. Castlereagh was determined not to allow a revised settlement to become too penal, although he realised that some additional penalties were inevitable. He enlisted the support of Alexander I with the argument that action should be taken 'not against France as a nation, but against France as a concentration of military Jacobinism' - the kind of vague and fairly meaningless sentiment perfectly calculated to appeal to the Tsar. The Tsar in turn won over Metternich and with that degree of unity, Castlereagh was able to resist the more excessive Prussian demands. In the end France had to agree to pay 700 million francs in compensation and to accept an army of occupation for five years. French borders were adjusted broadly back to where they had been in 1790, which meant losses in Belgium, on the Swiss border and Savoy. It was not as bad as Castlereagh (or the French themselves) had feared and at least Bonaparte was gone for good.

5 The Holy Alliance

On 25 May 1815, while Bonaparte was still in control of France, the Tsar produced a grand design for future European security. What he proposed was a personal pact between sovereigns and princes headed by Russia, Prussia and Austria. Other states would be invited to join these 'Holy Allies' in imposing moral and Christian principles in the diplomatic affairs of Europe. The ideas drafted by the Tsar in May were eventually translated into a formal alliance in September. As a document it was largely meaningless rubbish as Castlereagh noted in a despatch to Lord Liverpool in September 1815:

1 As soon as the instrument was executed between the Sovereigns, the Emperor of Russia brought it to me, developed his whole plan of universal peace, and told me the three Sovereigns had agreed to address a letter to the Prince Regent, to invite him to accede. Foreseeing the awk-
5 wardness of this piece of sublime mysticism and nonsense, especially to a British Sovereign, I examined with Prince Metternich every practical expedient to stop it; but when it reached me the deed was done and no other course remained than to do homage to the sentiment upon which it was founded, and to the advantages Europe might derive from three
10 such powerful Sovereigns directing all their influence to the preservation of peace ...

Metternich's first reaction to the Holy Alliance was much the same as that of Castlereagh. He referred to the details as 'a loud-sounding nothing'. However, he had already developed his own interpretation of legitimacy and his concern that revolutionary influences still lay below the surface ready to rise up and destroy European civilisation meant that he was open to any opportunity to increase the means of intervening against undesirable developments anywhere on the continent. This was something which Castlereagh knew could never be acceptable to British governments and especially to Parliament, where sympathy for demands for more liberal constitutions were likely to be strong. The Holy Alliance demonstrated to Castlereagh the urgency of the need for some more structured and precise set of commitments to be devised to defend the settlement. This he achieved within the next two months.

6 The Quadruple Alliance

Castlereagh's fears about the possible destructive effects of unrestrained interventionism only increased his determination to secure European stability by means of a more rational set of arrangements. In November 1815 he persuaded the allies to agree to a Quadruple Alliance which would run for twenty years. Under its terms the Bonaparte dynasty was to be excluded from France. The sixth article of the agreement provided for conferences to be held at intervals so that the allies could discuss their 'great common interests' and agree on any action that might be necessary 'for the maintenance of the peace of Europe'. This was the origin of the so-called 'Congress System'. Castlereagh saw this as an insurance that the dubious principles of the Holy Alliance would be kept in check. Metternich, on the other hand, saw it as a means of more effectively advancing the interventionist philosophy which he increasingly saw as vital to keeping liberal and revolutionary influences at bay. Thus though cooperation between Castlereagh and Metternich had become the fulcrum around which diplomacy was increasingly focused, in reality the two men were moving further apart with each development. Neither fully understood this at the time. Castlereagh believed that the Quadruple Alliance had effectively consigned the Holy Alliance to the background and that by means of regular congresses he would be able to monitor and influence decisions in the future, keeping the great powers 'in concert' and avoiding the need for intervention in the affairs of other countries unless the danger was clear and urgent. Metternich saw the congresses as offering the means by which agreement could be reached to nip undesirable developments in the bud and he was increasingly confident of his ability to manage the Tsar and enlist his support for this strategy.

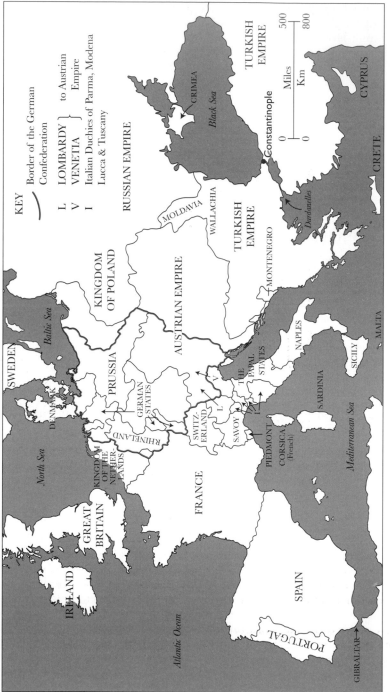

Europe in 1815

KEY

— Border of the German
Confederation

LOMBARDY ⎫ to Austrian
VENETIA ⎬ Empire

L
V
I Italian Duchies of Parma, Modena
Lucca & Tuscany

RUSSIAN EMPIRE

TURKISH
EMPIRE

CYPRUS

CRIMEA

Black Sea

Constantinople

CRETE

Dardanelles

MOLDAVIA

WALLACHIA

TURKISH
EMPIRE

MONTENEGRO

KINGDOM
OF POLAND

AUSTRIAN EMPIRE

500

800

Miles

Km

0

0

SWEDEN

Baltic Sea

PRUSSIA

GERMAN
STATES

NAPLES

MALTA

DENMARK

SWITZ-
ERLAND

L

V

THE
PAPAL
STATES

SICILY

North Sea

KINGDOM
OF THE
NETHER-
LANDS

RHINELAND

SAVOY

I

SARDINIA

GREAT
BRITAIN

FRANCE

PIEDMONT

CORSICA
(French)

Mediterranean Sea

IRELAND

Atlantic Ocean

SPAIN

PORTUGAL

GIBRALTAR

7 Castlereagh and the European Settlement - An Assessment

Any assessment of Castlereagh's achievements before and during the Congress of Vienna needs to take into account the following factors:

(i) Castlereagh had only limited control over the events as they developed in the final phases of the defeat of France.

(ii) He had to act generally in conformity with the wishes of the Prince Regent and the Cabinet and bear in mind the reaction to his policy in Parliament.

(iii) The extent of the demands for national recognition and unity (e.g. in Belgium or Italy) in 1815 was very limited.

(iv) Democratic and liberal ideas were not seen as constructive forces at that time - if anything the reverse was the case. The experience of the French Revolution had convinced most of Castlereagh's generation that constitutional changes were fraught with danger. In Britain many of those who were vocal in their support of constitutional progress in Europe were far less enthusiastic about changes at home.

(v) Britain desperately needed peace and - although that did not quite mean peace at any price - it did mean that the pressure was always on Castlereagh to find solutions and compromises.

(vi) Castlereagh was urgently needed by Liverpool's government in the House of Commons where he was almost alone as a major figure on the front bench. Most of the government's strength was in the House of Lords and Liverpool was constantly putting pressure on Castlereagh to conclude his work in Europe and get back home. The House of Commons was very independent and difficult to manage at the best of times and government majorities were far from certain even on important issues - only Castlereagh was really capable of managing the business of the House with some degree of efficiency. When he was away the Commons was often out of control. At one stage of the discussions he was compelled to return for a short time to London to sort out the chaos in the House, leaving Wellington in charge of affairs in Vienna.

Castlereagh was criticised after the Congress of Vienna for being too subservient to the interests of the great powers and was accused of being deceived and 'dazzled' by the likes of Metternich and Alexander I. This was partly a reflection of the reports of the grand dinners and balls which were regularly occurring in Vienna during the Congress. In fact Castlereagh found these kinds of social occasions tedious in the extreme. There is hardly any substance to the idea that his head was turned by the great figures around him. He regarded the Bourbons with near contempt. He accepted the power and position of the Tsar because it was a fact which could hardly be ignored but he looked on Alexander personally as an erratic and potentially dangerous man who had to be carefully managed and occasionally shown a firm hand. He respected Metternich as an equal - not as a mentor - and that respect was returned by the Austrian, who, despite some difficult periods in the years ahead, continued to regard his relationship with Castlereagh as the most important element in Austrian diplomacy.

Particular anger was focused on Castlereagh over what the Whigs and radicals in Britain saw as his preference for the rights of auto-cratic monarchs over the claims of constitutionalists in Europe. However, much of this hostility was misconceived. There is no doubt, of course, that Castlereagh was deeply distrustful of anything that smacked of democratic or even overly liberal ideas - anything in short which could be interpreted as revolutionary or likely to stimulate revolutionary tendencies. But this was far from meaning that he was opposed to moderate constitutional concessions. When the Spanish Bourbon, King Ferdinand VII, was restored in 1814, Castlereagh applauded the end of the 1812 constitution which he saw as far too democratic, but opposed the total restoration of autocratic rule, hoping for a sensible compromise. He supported the moderate constitutional experiments in France, Holland and Sweden on the grounds that the loyalty of the people would improve and this would be good for stability. It should always be remembered that on the great domestic constitutional issue in Britain - Catholic Emancipation - Castlereagh had stood resolutely on the side of reform for years and had even resigned from the government back in 1801 over the failure to provide for this in the Act of Union between Great Britain and Ireland. Castlereagh's reputation as a reactionary was ill-deserved.

The same considerations apply to the other great charge levelled against Castlereagh and the settlement in general - that of disre-garding the rights of nationalities. This was a charge based more on hindsight than on contemporary evidence. In 1815 there was little opposition in Belgium to the arrangements made for Belgian union with Holland. This was an experiment which could well have worked effectively had it not been for the stupidity and prejudice of the Dutch King in the years which followed. Similarly, there was in Italy almost no sign of the fervent national feelings which were to arise in the years ahead. Italian nationalism was a negligible factor even in the revolts which occurred in 1820-1. In 1815 the arrangements made for Italy were based on the wider strategic implications. This was far from unreasonable given the situation at the time. A more serious claim to national status was represented by the Poles, who, until comparatively recently, had enjoyed their own independent status. However, as we have seen, there was little in reality that Castlereagh could have done for the Poles. They had already lost their independence before the era of Bonaparte and nothing could have dislodged the Tsar from Poland short of an all-out war against him by all the other powers, who then would have had no basis of agreement about how to settle the Polish Question. Neither Austria nor Prussia would have agreed to the resurrection of a Polish state.

Any reasonable assessment of Castlereagh's conduct from 1812 to 1815 must reach the conclusion that he achieved as much as was practicably possible both to safeguard British interests and to provide for a stabilised Europe. To Castlereagh these two things were inseparable since there was no more fundamental British interest than the maintenance of peace. To achieve his aims he often courted the displeasure of his Cabinet colleagues and even his chief, Lord Liverpool. For example, in early 1815 the Cabinet would have caved in totally to Alexander I over Poland rather than risk war - it was Castlereagh who insisted that the Tsar must make concessions. He even concluded a secret treaty of alliance with the French against the possibility of having to resist the Tsar by force - to the horror of Liverpool and his colleagues. Then again, to secure the Tsar's fuller cooperation, Castlereagh undertook, entirely on his own responsibility, that Britain would take over a number of Russian debts - the Treasury was not impressed.

The final point of assessment should be to consider the extent to which Castlereagh, in pursuing what he saw as a rational and constructive policy, within the limits of practicability, moved beyond the narrow insular outlook of his colleagues in London and particularly the attitudes in Parliament. Recognising the need for European cooperation he came to view the interests of Britain within the context of the wider issues in Europe and in particular recognised that Britain needed to be trusted as well as respected. On the other hand, he failed completely to convey to his contemporaries the ideas which underpinned his policy. He was a notoriously poor speaker and, in any case, regarded popular acclaim and open diplomacy with contempt. Only the Duke of Wellington, who was on the continent throughout the final stages of the struggle against Bonaparte and replaced Castlereagh at Vienna for a short time, really understood and appreciated the soundness of the policies he adopted and the qualities of patience, skill and courage with which he pursued them.

Making notes on 'Britain and the European Settlement'

This chapter provides the essential starting point for studying events in the period up to 1865. Your notes should focus on:
a) What were the most urgent requirements Britain had in relation to the settlement?
b) What problems and other considerations limited Castlereagh's freedom of action at Vienna?
c) What were the main terms which affected British interests?
d) Make a list of what you would see as the main strengths and main weaknesses of the final decisions made at Vienna.
e) Make a note to review the Vienna Settlement as you study later developments so that you can assess the impact which the settlement had in subsequent years.
The above could also serve usefully as discussion points.

Answering essay questions on 'Britain and the European Settlement'

It is rare for exam essays in British history (i.e. as opposed to European history) to focus wholly on Britain and the Vienna Settlement. It is much more likely that you would be required to fit this material into a broader question dealing with Castlereagh's foreign policy generally. Examples of these are given at the end of Chapter 3.

However, you may well encounter the use of structured questions in the examinations you take. In these you are required to answer a series of shorter questions, often with an emphasis on factual recall, on a given theme. The points mentioned above as study notes/discussion points might well serve as the basis for shorter questions such as these.

Source-based questions on 'Britain and the European Settlement'

1. Castlereagh's despatch to the British Ambassador in Russia (September 1813)
Read the extract on pages 18-19 and answer the following questions.
a) What does Castlereagh mean by 'a peace concluded in concert'? (5 marks)
b) What does he see as the advantages of such a peace? (5 marks)
c) To what extent do Castlereagh's arguments suggest that he was concerned about the solidarity of the alliance? (10 marks)

2. Pitt's Memorandum (January 1805)
Read the extract on pages 22-3 and answer the following questions.
a) In your own words explain how Pitt sees future peace and stability being achieved in Europe. (5 marks)
b) Compare Castlereagh's despatch of September 1813 with Pitt's

Memorandum. In what ways is Pitt's influence shown in
Castlereagh's comments? (5 marks)
c) What similarities and differences can you detect between Pitt's
ideas and the eventual arrangements made at Vienna?
(10 marks)

3. *The Holy Alliance (1815)*
Read the extract on pages 28 and answer the following questions.
a) What does this letter tell us about Castlereagh's attitude to the
Tsar and his relations with Metternich? (5 marks)
b) Why was Castlereagh particularly concerned about the invitation
to the Prince Regent to sign the Holy Alliance? (5 marks)

Summary Diagram
Britain and the European Settlement - 1815

1812: Formation of Allied Coalition against France

Treaty of Chaumont set out principles for a future settlement

Domestic Affairs

Economic and financial crisis for British government due to the accumulated costs of fighting wars and supporting allies since 1793

1813-14: Fall of the Napoleonic Empire

First Peace of Paris offered lenient terms to France

1814-15: Congress of Vienna

Return and second defeat of Napoleon

Second Peace of Paris imposed tougher terms on France

Tsar proposed the 'Holy Alliance'

Castlereagh countered with the Quadruple Alliance and the concept of congress diplomacy

3 Castlereagh, Canning and the Maintenance of the European Settlement, 1815-30

Between 1815 and 1830, British foreign policy was dominated by the aim of ensuring that the peace settlement agreed at Vienna was maintained. The maintenance of the settlement was fundamental to British interests because it was perceived as the best guarantee against a resumption of war, which the British economy and financial system could ill afford. Castlereagh, a principal architect of the settlement as we have seen in Chapter 2, remained Foreign Secretary until August 1822, when, exhausted by overwork and mentally unstable, he took his own life. He was succeeded by George Canning. Canning was a brilliant politician who had already served as Foreign Secretary from 1807 to 1809 when he had come close to becoming Prime Minister. He remained at the Foreign Office until April 1827, when he briefly succeeded Lord Liverpool as Prime Minister, dying later the same year. Foreign policy then became the responsibility of Lord Aberdeen, who served as Foreign Secretary from 1828 to 1830 in the Duke of Wellington's government.

Although the people making and carrying out policy changed, the fundamental aim of maintaining peace and stability in Europe remained constant. The extent to which the principles and methods of these men (and in particular those of Castlereagh and Canning), differed, became a subject of debate both for their contemporaries and, subsequently, for historians (see pages 126-7). However, what unquestionably did change were the circumstances in which policy was conducted. By 1830 the assumptions on which some of the decisions made at Vienna were based had been proved unfounded, whilst in some cases the actual circumstances had changed so much that the arrangements made in 1815 could no longer be sustained. This meant that, in practice, British policy sometimes had to focus on preserving the spirit of the settlement rather than always insisting on preserving the strict letter of the Vienna terms.

There were three key changes in the situation in Europe with which British foreign policy had to cope.

a) The Position of France

In 1815 France was the defeated giant which had destabilised Europe for over two decades. Curtailing the power of France and insuring Europe against a resurgence of French expansionism had been the central problem facing the victorious allies at Vienna. By 1818 France had effectively been restored to equal diplomatic status with the other great powers. As will be seen in more detail below, by 1820 countries like Russia and Austria were urging that France should be allowed to send troops into Spain to put down the 'revolutionary' influences there. This was a development which Britain, whose forces had spent years expelling the French from Spain during the Napoleonic Wars, found unacceptable. Even so, the fact of France's re-emergence on the diplomatic scene was not in itself something which Britain saw as negative - after all it had also been central to Castlereagh's policy that France should not be too weakened or permanently alienated. In fact it was at Castlereagh's suggestion that France was invited to the Congress of Aix-la-Chapelle in 1818 where French diplomatic isolation was officially ended.

b) The Emergence of Nationalism

In 1815 nationalism had been an issue of little or no consequence to the great powers. However, between 1815 and 1830 the underlying strength of nationalist feeling in various parts of Europe became increasingly apparent. During this period movements started in Germany and Italy which were to lead to these two countries becoming unified sovereign states in the second half of the century. There were revolts in numerous Italian states in 1820-21 and in Greece in 1821. These were only the most prominent revolts - the ones which most directly involved Britain. For example, the Greek revolt against the Turks was only one of a series of rebellions within the Turkish Empire in which an ethnic group attempted to establish its own national state. Nationalism was also at work in the German states. There were no actual revolts there in 1820-21, but this was only because the Prussians, acting under Metternich's influence, had already introduced a repressive system in 1819 to counteract evidence of growing unrest. However, these measures merely held back the pressures for a time. When, in 1830, further revolts broke out all over Europe (see below), there were rebellions in some of the German states and also in the Netherlands, where Belgian resentment against the Dutch had been simmering since 1815. Revolts such as these proved a major problem for the great powers, not least because they could not always agree on how to respond.

c) The Growth of Liberalism

The revolts outlined above did not result purely from nationalistic feelings, but often stemmed from general resentment against some imperial overlord, or, as in the case of the Netherlands, an oppressive majority group. The French Revolution had unleashed a widespread critical approach to political systems which had not previously existed. All over Europe there was a growing demand for the introduction of constitutional forms of government which would bring an end to absolutist repression without involving the total, revolutionary overthrow of traditional monarchical rule. Nowhere was this desire for constitutionalism of a moderate and limited kind more clear than amongst the educated middle classes. In Britain the years from 1815 to 1830 saw the growing demand for parliamentary reform which culminated in the reform crisis of 1831-2 and the passing of the Reform Act of 1832. In Britain, of course, there was already a limited monarchy and a representative system in which even some members of the working classes had the vote - 1832 merely saw a rationalising and cautious extension of political rights. Elsewhere in Europe a demand for a constitution of any kind was, in some cases, tantamount to a revolution - at least in the eyes of absolute monarchs. Even those countries which had constitutions, such as France from 1815, generally had arrangements so limited and ineffectual that they were quite inadequate to meet the aspirations of the increasingly wealthy and intelligent middling classes. These business and professional classes, whilst not aiming for anything approaching democracy - they were too wary of the increasing numbers of the working classes for that - were nevertheless anxious to establish political systems which would protect and advance their own interests. The conflicts which emerged between monarchs and constitutionalists, inspired by liberal and/or national aspirations, challenged from time to time the arrangements which the great powers had made in 1815. Liberalism was especially strong in the western half of Europe.

1 The Congress System, 1815-22

The origin of the idea of long-term organised collaboration between the great powers for the maintenance of stability in Europe lay in the strategy of William Pitt as carried forward by Castlereagh in the Treaty of Chaumont in 1814. At the Congress of Vienna, Castlereagh used the Chaumont commitment to secure future collaboration as the basis of the Quadruple Alliance of 1815, under Article VI of which the four powers, Britain, Russia, Austria and Prussia, agreed to meet at 'fixed periods' to consult upon their 'common interests' and on 'measures which at each of these periods shall be considered the most salutary for the prosperity of Nations, and for the Peace of Europe'. Three things are clear about Castlereagh's intentions in 1815 as regards the role of future congresses:

(i) that they should act primarily as a means of communication between the powers to maintain closer relations, avoid misunderstandings and anticipate possible areas of conflict;

(ii) that they should be used as a means of securing agreement for joint action to interfere in the affairs of other states only as a last resort in situations where the peace of Europe was clearly at risk; and

(iii) that he saw congresses only as a useful addition to the existing means of conducting diplomacy and not as having some

overriding authority to determine and impose a consensus for
action - that is to say, he held Britain's right to determine British
policy in the last resort to be unaltered.

Before looking at the actual congresses which took place between
1815 and 1822 there are some further background points which
need to be borne in mind. First, the whole question of the
Quadruple Alliance was subject to the ratification of Parliament. The
House of Commons, mindful of the need to prevent any further
trouble from France, approved the Alliance proposals in 1815 by a
sizeable majority, but even at that stage the idea of a peacetime
alliance with the 'despotic' sovereigns of Europe came in for heavy
criticism from some MPs who argued that such a system was a threat
to liberty in Europe and even perhaps in Britain. There was a
General Election in 1818 and the mood of the new House, with the
war receding into the past, was much more critical of the idea of a
permanent system of conferences. Liverpool expressed the opinion
in 1818 that, if the terms of the Quadruple Alliance had had to be
put to the new House at that point, approval would almost certainly
not have been given. In addition, the Cabinet itself grew increasingly
apprehensive about the Alliance. Canning returned to the Cabinet in
1816 and, although he now held a relatively minor office, he had
great influence with Liverpool, with whom he had been a close
friend for many years. Canning was very critical, in particular, of the
'fixed periods' proposed for conferences under Article VI of the
Alliance which he described as 'new' and 'highly questionable'. It
should also be noted that Castlereagh himself became concerned, as
early as 1818, that the regular meetings he had envisaged might be
used for purposes of which he could not approve. This was brought
sharply into focus for him by the discussions of a conference of
ambassadors which had been set up in Paris to discuss various aspects
of the peace terms with France, such as the duration for which allied
troops should continue to occupy France and the schedule under
which the French should make the payment of reparations imposed
under the Second Peace of Paris. Both Metternich and the Tsar regularly tried to expand the areas of discussion beyond the strict issues
directly affecting France and this convinced Castlereagh that it might
be better to abandon the idea of scheduled meetings in favour of
meetings called only necessary to deal with limited, clearly defined
matters.

a) The Congress of Aix-la-Chapelle, 1818

This was the only Congress, of the series held up to 1822, which met
the conditions and served the purposes which Castlereagh had originally envisaged. It was, in fact, the only Congress which he actually
attended in person. The conference was called to consider the posi-

tion of France and to decide on its re-admission to the diplomatic fold. As indicated above, Castlereagh was anxious that France should attend the conference and end its isolation. He was keen to do this because he saw France, provided it was stable and unaggressive, as a useful counterpoise to the unpredictability of the Tsar. The Congress itself was relatively uncontroversial. The allies duly agreed to withdraw their armies of occupation and all outstanding questions to do with reparation payments were settled. France was admitted into a new 'Quintuple Alliance' system for the maintenance of peace in Europe which entitled it to attend any future congresses. Meantime the Quadruple Alliance itself was to be maintained as a guarantee of continued French good behaviour. Castlereagh obtained an important modification of Article VI. Future congresses were not to be held at fixed intervals, but, as he explained to the cabinet:

1 The eventual reunions are strictly limited to those interests that grow out of the ... maintenance of peace by the existing treaties, and, instead of declaring any intention that such reunions shall be held at fixed periods, as the Sixth Article provides shall be the case, it is expressly
5 declared that they shall be special, namely that they shall arise out of the occasion and be agreed upon by the five Courts [i.e. Britain, Russia, Austria, Prussia and France] at the time; in fact, no Power can be considered as pledged ... to any meeting whatever.

This arrangement was entirely in accord with Castlereagh's own wishes - it was certainly good news to the Cabinet. Even so, the fear that Britain might be dragged into some kind of conflict in Europe remained strong in British government circles. When a military revolt broke out in Spain in January 1820 these fears intensified. The leaders of the revolt claimed that its purpose was to restore constitutional government and this was more than enough to provoke demands for a conference from Russia, France and Prussia with the object of discussing how the 'revolution' could be put down. Accordingly, Castlereagh was asked by the Cabinet to state his views on British policy towards intervention in Spain. The result was a 'State Paper' produced in May 1820, in which Castlereagh dealt not only with the question of Spain but defined British policy towards the whole question of intervention in the internal affairs of other countries in general.

b) Castlereagh's State Paper of May 1820

The State Paper was a secret document which was initially only circulated to British ambassadors and the governments of the great powers. Castlereagh was determined to prevent any great-power intervention in Spain, partly because British public opinion was overwhelmingly favourable to the revolt, and partly because Spain was seen as a neutral buffer state on important British trade routes. He therefore firmly quashed the idea of a congress and stressed the argument that intervention in Spain would be fraught with difficulties and unlikely to end in success since the Spanish would fight it tooth and nail. To support this view he cited the opinion and experience of the Duke of Wellington who knew only too well from the Peninsular Campaigns that 'the Spanish Nation is of all the European People that which will least brook any interference from abroad'. However, the example of Spain served to allow Castlereagh to develop a much more general set of principles in relation to British attitudes towards intervention:

1   The King of Great Britain, from the nature of our Constitution has ... to acquire all his means [i.e. money] through Parliament, and ... in a War which the Voice of the Country does not support, the efforts of the strongest administration which ever served the Crown would soon be
5   unequal to the prosecution of the contest ... In Great Britain ... sentiment runs strongly against the late policy of the King of Spain ... We cannot conceal from ourselves how generally the acts of the King of Spain since his restoration have rendered his government unpopular and how impossible it would be to reconcile the People of England to
10 the use of force ... for the purpose of replacing power in his hands ... The principle of one State interfering by force in the internal affairs of another, in order to enforce obedience to the governing authority, is always a question of the greatest possible moral as well as political delicacy ... to generalize such a principle and to think of reducing it to a
15 System, or to impose it as an obligation, is a scheme utterly impractical and objectionable ... No country having a Representative System of Government could act upon it and the sooner such doctrine shall be distinctly abjured as forming in any degree the basis of our Alliance the better ...

c) The Congress of Troppau, 1820

This Congress opened in October 1820. That year had already seen revolts break out in Spain, Portugal and the Kingdom of Naples, which then comprised the whole of southern Italy including Sicily (see the map on page 30). Metternich's reaction to these revolts was predictable - he wanted to see them put down. Most of all he wished to crush the revolt in Naples since this lay directly within what had been accepted in 1815 as an Austrian sphere of influence. Castlereagh's reaction was equally predictable. He refused to regard the revolts as collectively constituting an unacceptable threat to European stability, preferring to analyse them as separate issues - each to be assessed on its own merits. In Castlereagh's view the troubles in Spain and Portugal were the result of poor government in those countries and the revolts there were to some degree understandable. On the other hand, he believed that the Kingdom of

Naples had been well-governed on the whole, and that therefore Austria would be justified in intervening to put down the rebels.

Castlereagh was prepared to give secret moral and diplomatic support to Austria and he communicated this to Metternich as early as July 1820, not long after the 'Neapolitan revolt' started. This was not a position adopted by Castlereagh in isolation. It commanded general Cabinet support, including that of Canning. However, what Castlereagh was strongly opposed to was any public British support for armed intervention against the rebels and this meant he also opposed the idea of calling a congress to discuss collective action by the Alliance against any of the revolts. Such a congress would bring the question of intervention right into the public arena and this was something the government could not really afford in 1820. The problem was that Liverpool's government was desperately unpopular. Mounting social and political unrest resulting from economic recession had culminated in the infamous 'Peterloo massacre' in 1819, following which the government had felt compelled to resort to a series of repressive measures. In 1820 this already volatile situation had been made worse by the scandal which resulted from the King's determination to divorce his wife Queen Caroline, a process which required approval by Parliament which was not forthcoming. There was every chance that the government might fall before the year was out. The last thing Castlereagh (who, it must be remembered, was Leader of the House of Commons as well as Foreign Secretary) needed was a controversy over intervention against constitutionalists on behalf of absolutism.

Unfortunately for Castlereagh's policy, Metternich wanted more than secret moral support from Britain. He feared revolutionary upheavals, but he also feared the vulnerability of Austria and did not wish to act alone. All his instincts told him to ensure that he could count on the support of Russia as well as Britain, especially since the Tsar had a track record of sudden and unpredictable bouts of liberal feelings which might occur at any time and in any context other than Russia itself. Metternich knew that in the last resort he could not act without Russian agreement. He could not be sure of the Russian position without a full-scale Alliance conference since this was something for which the Tsar had been pressing for some time and he would not commit himself to anything without. France also wanted a conference, in its case because of the revolt in neighbouring Spain which it wished to crush by armed force. This was something it could not risk doing without the approval of the Alliance powers. Metternich would have preferred to deal directly with the Tsar over Naples but it was not an option open to him. He knew, of course, that the British government was in deep trouble in domestic affairs and that Castlereagh might not even be Foreign Secretary much longer. For Metternich, the Congress of Troppau was an unavoidable necessity.

What was also unavoidable was that Castlereagh should distance

Britain from the proceedings. The Government could not contemplate, in the circumstances of 1820, becoming associated with a policy of intervention against constitutionalists. Castlereagh was caught in a dilemma over Troppau: without his presence there was a greater risk of decisions being made which were unacceptable to Britain; yet attending the conference was out of the question given the attitude in the House of Commons. In any case Castlereagh could not have been spared from the Commons at that point. He was virtually the only government figure with any authority in the House, Canning having been out of the country for much of 1820 due to his opposition to the government's policy towards Queen Caroline. In the end Castlereagh opted to send an 'observer' to Troppau, a decision which did not in the event leave Britain as isolated as Castlereagh had feared since the French rather surprisingly elected to do the same thing.

The Congress of Troppau produced a protocol (i.e. a formal statement of diplomatic agreement) signed by Russia, Prussia and Austria which reaffirmed the right of those countries to overthrow, by force if necessary, any revolutionary government which they considered a danger to other states:

The Troppau Protocol

1. States, forming part of the European Alliance, which have undergone a change, due to revolution, in the form of their constitution and the results of which menace other States, ipso facto cease to be part of the Alliance and remain excluded from it, until their situation gives guarantees of legal order and stability.
2. The Allied Powers do not limit themselves to announcing this exclusion; but faithful to the principles which they have proclaimed and to the respect due to the authority of every legitimate government as to every act emanating from its own free will, agree to refuse rcognition to changes brought about by illegal methods.
3. When States where such changes have been made, cause by their proximity other countries to fear immediate danger, and when the Allied Powers can exercise effective and beneficial action towards them, they will employ, in order to bring them back to the bosom of the Alliance, first friendly representation, secondly measures of coercion, if the employment of such coercion is indispensable.

This statement of a general principle of intervention in the internal affairs of other countries angered Castlereagh but did not really surprise him. It was precisely the kind of grand-scale scheme set in high-flown language which the Tsar loved. Metternich's need for Russian support to deal with the situation in Italy had left him with little choice but to play up to the Tsar and oversee the drafting of a set of proposals the sweeping nature of which even he did not really approve. Castlereagh was forced by the Troppau Protocol into a move which he greatly disliked. He felt compelled to use extracts from the May Paper in a series of despatches to ambassadors to rebut the Protocol. He flatly rejected all claims to any right of intervention in the affairs of other nations unless motivated by self-defence, which, he argued, could not be defined in advance but only as events unfolded. He warned that the Protocol was a threat to the liberties of Europe which might be abused by unscrupulous rulers in the future, and concluded by arguing that it was against both international law and the British constitution, as well as being totally impractical. These views, most uncharacteristically for Castlereagh, were published in January 1821 because the government knew well enough that it could not afford to leave the Troppau Protocol unchallenged given the hostile attitude in the House of Commons.

d) The Decline of the Congress System

The Congress of Troppau was adjourned to Laibach (now known as Ljubljana in modern-day Slovenia), where it continued in January 1821. Castlereagh sent his brother, Lord Stewart, the British Ambassador at Vienna to represent Britain this time. Affairs were now dominated by the long-awaited Austrian intervention in Italy where the revolt in Naples was crushed along with a more recent revolt which had occurred in Piedmont. By the middle of April the problems in Italy had been resolved and the way was open for better relations between Castlereagh and Metternich, something both statesmen urgently desired. The chances of renewed collaboration were enhanced by the news of revolts in the Balkan territories of the Turkish Empire, the most serious of which involved the Greeks (see Chapter 5). Trouble in the Turkish Empire raised the possibility of Russian intervention on behalf of fellow Slavs and/or fellow Orthodox Christians, something both Castlereagh and Metternich wished to avoid.

Meanwhile, the question of the future of Spain still remained unresolved. The Congress at Laibach had failed to clarify anything beyond the fact that the European powers were divided over the issue. Leading French politicians were not fully in agreement over intervention in Spain, though the majority were keen on the idea; the Tsar urgently wanted intervention; Metternich was reluctant once the Italian revolts were put down; Britain remained implacably opposed. Castlereagh hoped to isolate the Tsar by reaching an agreement with Metternich and persuading the French against taking any action in Spain without Anglo-Austrian approval. What he urgently needed was a face-to-face meeting with Metternich to try to work out a joint approach to both the Spanish and Greek problems. The opportunity arose towards the end of 1821 with a visit that October by George IV to Hanover as its new King. This state occasion gave Castlereagh and Metternich the perfect setting for what turned out to be their last meeting.

The meeting was a success in the sense that both men left Hanover with a feeling of accord about their ultimate goals. They reached no specific agreements about tactics in relation to Spain, but did agree to jointly apply pressure on the Tsar against any war between Russia and Turkey over the Greek Question, even though they were not totally in agreement on this question either. Over the winter of 1821-2 both men, in C.J. Bartlett's words, 'dedicated themselves to their desks', writing lengthy despatches 'replete with every conceivable argument in favour of peace'. Metternich argued that intervention by Russia in Greece would reduce the allies' ability to respond to problems elsewhere such as Spain, Portugal and even France, where doubts about the stability of the restored Bourbon dynasty were never far from the surface. Castlereagh expressed doubts about the ability of the Greeks to govern themselves and insisted that even if they could, the experiment would not be worth the devastation which could result from a European war.

Largely at the insistence of the Tsar, yet another Congress was scheduled to be held at Verona in September 1822. Castlereagh agreed to attend this Congress and also to go to a preliminary meeting in Vienna. He hoped at this meeting to lay the groundwork for a solution to the Greek crisis based on autonomy for the Greeks within the Turkish Empire and a general agreement against intervention in Spain. He hoped that this would be a joint Anglo-Austrian position which the Tsar would have to accept. In the event, however, Castlereagh was never to leave for Vienna. He committed suicide on 12 August 1822, his mind apparently having become unhinged by the enormous burdens of work he had been carrying for so many years. There have been many theories about what finally provoked his demise. He had been known to be highly strung and sensitive to criticism for many years. It has also been suggested that he was being blackmailed over a false allegation that he had been involved in homosexual practice. According to one source, his dislike of public speaking led him to use ether, as a stimulant, before making speeches. If this is true then this may conceivably have played a part in his mental deterioration. Whatever the truth of the matter, his death marked the end of any diplomatic initiatives based on Anglo-Austrian collaboration. Metternich's regard for Castlereagh's abilities and his trust in their friendship seems only to have been exceeded by his distaste for the man who was to be his successor.

2 George Canning (1770-1827)

Like Castlereagh, Canning had an Irish background rooted in the Ulster gentry. His father (also George) originally came from a wealthy family but fell out badly with his own father who ended up disinheriting him. Canning's father came to London (with only a small annual allowance to live on) and eventually qualified as a lawyer. However, he showed little interest in following his profession and dabbled more in politics and writing. He married poorly in the sense that his bride had even less money than he had, so his son George's prospects were inauspicious from the start. The elder George then compounded the bleakness of his family's prospects by dying little more than a year after his son's birth. Canning's mother received only meagre support from her father-in-law and was forced to take to the stage as a career to support herself and her child. Acting was a distinctly dubious means of earning a living for a woman in those days and George Canning might have lived and died in total obscurity, had not his grandfather softened in his attitude. When Canning was eight years old his grandfather suddenly agreed to make adequate provision for the boy's education and maintenance. He was sent to live with his uncle, Stratford Canning, who had also come to London and had built up a comfortable business. Canning therefore was 'rescued' from an itinerant lifestyle of the provincial touring theatre and deposited in a highly respectable prep school. At the age of 12 he moved on to Eton and from there in 1787 to Oxford University.

Eton and Oxford gave Canning access to social advancement and the political world. The public schools and universities were a recruiting ground for young men of talent, even those without their own money, into the political world and there was no doubting Canning's ability as a scholar and public speaker. He soon came to the attention of the Prime Minister, William Pitt, who eventually arranged for Canning to enter the House of Commons in 1793 sitting for a borough on the Isle of Wight. This was a crucial connection, for Canning, although now well-educated, had very little money and could never have afforded to finance his own election to Parliament. By the end of 1795 he had been appointed to an Under-Secretaryship at the Foreign Office and his (paid) politcal career was underway. It was a career which promised brilliance from the start. In many ways it turned out to be a career unfulfilled. Canning rose quickly under Pitt towards the leading rank of politicians. He married an heiress with a considerable fortune and by 1807, a year after Pitt's death, he was Foreign Secretary. In 1809 he was a credible candidate for Prime Minister, though in the event the post went to Spencer Percival. In the same year a clash with his Cabinet colleague Castlereagh over war policy led to the two men fighting a pistol duel in which Canning was slightly injured. The scandal kept both men out of office until 1812, when Canning's reluctance to compromise with Castlereagh led to his exclusion from a reconstructed government under Percival and then, following the assassination of the Prime Minister, under Lord Liverpool. When Liverpool's government was formed Castlereagh, who was already Foreign Secretary and Leader of the Commons offered to give up the Foreign Office to Canning in order to strengthen the Cabinet. In the event Canning refused to accept

Castlereagh's leadership in the Commons since he could not bring himself to acknowledge that he would be the subordinate - this intransigence left him out of office altogether and Castlereagh in possession of both posts.

Canning returned to office in 1816, forced to take a junior Cabinet appointment simply to resurrect his political career. His close friendship with Lord Liverpool and his personal abilities made him more important in the Cabinet than his job (President of the Indian Board) would normally have allowed, but his career was thrown off track again in 1820 when he felt compelled to resign owing to his opposition to the government's policy in relation to Queen Caroline. He would probably never have returned to office at all had it not been for the suicide of Castlereagh in August 1822. Canning had already accepted the lucrative post of Governor-General of India through which he hoped to restore his wife's original fortune which had dwindled alarmingly during the years of their marriage. With Castlereagh's death Liverpool was able to offer Canning both the offices left vacant by Castlereagh.

All through his career Canning stood unswervingly for the policy of granting Roman Catholics the right to sit in Parliament - something denied them by the wording of the Parliamentary Oath which contained denunciations of essential Catholic doctrine. In this he was in agreement with Castlereagh but at odds with Liverpool, Peel and Wellington. This stance was also opposed by both George III and George IV. In the case of the latter, Canning also suffered from persistent rumours (probably untrue) that he had once been a lover of Queen Caroline, rumours given more credence by his support for her in the crisis of 1820-21. As Foreign Secretary from 1822 he was widely expected to pursue a policy more independent from the other European powers and more liberal in attitude towards those movements in Europe which sought to promote constitutionalism over absolutism.

3 The End of the Congress System

The arrival of Canning at the Foreign Office in 1822 was regarded by most contemporaries as marking a great change in British policy. Metternich certainly saw it this way. To him Canning was a dangerous radical who could not be trusted and his reaction to Castlereagh's suicide was to realign Austria more closely with Russia. In Britain the critics of Castlereagh hoped for an approach which would detach policy from what was perceived to be the damaging influence of the continentals.

i The discerning mind of Mr Canning will doubtless draw true and most useful conclusions from the scene which has passed before him. He is not personally connected with any of the Foreign Courts, nor person-

ally pledged to their measures. The adoption of a new line of policy by
5 him does not carry with it the painful acknowledgement that his former
system had been wrong.

(From *Observations on the Appointment of the Rt. Hon. George Canning* by
Lewis Goldsmith, published 1822.)

Canning certainly had no interest in an allied approach to solving the
Greek Question. He believed that this would have to be dealt with
through direct negotiations with the Russians and Turks. Similarly, in
the case of Spain, he saw that Britain needed to come to some agreement with France over what action, if any, was to be taken. Canning
therefore placed little importance on the discussions at Verona. This
Congress was attended by Wellington on behalf of Britain. There had
been a delay of about a month between Castlereagh's death and
Canning's appointment, brought about mainly by the King's opposition to Canning coming back to the Cabinet, but partly by his own
doubts - the attractions of the great fortune he could have made in
India being very strong. During the interim, the Cabinet asked
Wellington to go to Verona and by the time Canning had settled into
the Foreign Office he was already on his way.

The absence of Castlereagh from the Verona Conference made it
virtually certain that nothing concrete would be agreed. Wellington's
fame as a soldier had made him just about the most famous man in all
Europe at this time. His prestige in Britain was at a level probably
unequalled before or since. For the rest of his life he exercised an
influence of incredible proportions politically. However, all this was
unimpressive to Metternich who had no faith whatsoever in
Wellington as a diplomat. He made sure that Wellington was excluded
from the most crucial discussions on the Spanish Question and virtually ignored his contributions in other areas. Nevertheless, Wellington
did enough in Verona to eliminate any lingering prospect there might
have been of joint allied action in Spain. If there was to be intervention in the future it would come unilaterally from France - that much
was clear. When Wellington departed from Verona at the end of
November, the Congress System was effectively dead.

4 Spain, Portugal and the 'New World'

The outcome of the Verona Congress (or rather the lack of an
outcome!) suited Canning. He hoped to deter the French from any
intervention in Spain, but he realised that with the threat of revolutionary ideas so close to them across the Pyrenees this might prove
impossible. Ultimately, Canning, like Castlereagh, was not prepared
to go to war over the ultra-democratic Spanish constitution, of which
he thoroughly disapproved. When the French finally invaded Spain in
April 1823 to overthrow the 1812 constitution and restore the abso-

'John Bull dressed as a British officer goes to the rescue of Portugal, his country's ancient ally'

lutist King Ferdinand, Canning announced to the House of Commons that Britain intended to remain neutral in the conflict. It was a different matter altogether in the case of Portugal. Any possibility of French intervention in Spain being carried on into Portugal was totally unacceptable. There was a further point at issue. Except for Brazil, which was Portuguese, most of Central and South America had been under Spanish control for more than three centuries. During the European Wars Spain's grip on these imperial territories had become fragile. In many areas independence movements had sprung up and in some cases independence had actually been declared. Brazil had also declared itself independent in December 1822. To British interests these territories represented important markets and sources of natural resources for the future. It suited Britain therefore to champion the rights of Central and South American states to their freedom. Canning was determined that if intervention in Spain had to be tolerated then it should be made quite clear that rights over Spanish imperial possessions were not included in any French occupation.

a) Spain and the Spanish Colonies

Here Canning achieved his objective by his preferred method of direct negotiation with France. In October 1823, he concluded an agreement which came to be known as the Polignac Memorandum after the Prince de Polignac, the French Ambassador in London. The French agreed that their intervention in Spain would not be extended to the colonies. With this settled, Canning opened up discussions with the Americans with the aim of securing a joint Anglo-American declaration against any future European interference with what were now, in effect, independent former Spanish colonies. This Canning did not achieve since the American President, James Monroe, who originally favoured the idea, was persuaded by his Secretary of State (the equivalent of Foreign Minister) to issue his own unilateral statement in December 1823, insisting that the Americas were no longer open to European (i.e. including British) colonisation - the so-called 'Monroe Doctrine'. Canning responded to this by publishing the Polignac Memorandum to demonstrate to the South Americans that it pre-dated the Monroe Doctrine. This also underlined the fact that whatever the Monroe Doctrine implied about the power of the USA, it was in reality the British Navy which ruled the waves and would be in effect the guarantor of South American independence. Canning followed this by initially recognising some of the more stable South American governments such as those of Mexico, Argentina and Columbia - a general recognition of all the Spanish states of South America came at the end of 1824. In Canning's own words he had 'called the New World into existence to redress the balance of the Old'.

b) Portugal

Here Canning was forced into intervention in order to carry out his policy. The fact that this seemed at odds with the general attitude of the British government towards intervention was explained by Canning in terms of the 'special relationship' that could be argued to exist between the two countries, based on the fact that Britain had been pledged to defend Portugal against foreign aggression since the seventeenth century - a pledge which had been honoured on several occasions in the eighteenth century as well as in the Napoleonic Wars. Portugal was convulsed internally by a conflict between the constitutionalist King John, who favoured a limited parliamentary system, and his absolutist-minded younger son Dom Miguel who staged a coup in February 1824. Canning, disapproving of absolutism as much as he did of democracy and fearing that Miguel would become a French puppet, ordered the British forces stationed in Portugal to restore King John to his throne. In 1825, continuing his 'New World' policy, Canning persuaded John to recognise the independence of Brazil as a separate state with John's elder son and heir, Dom Pedro (who had headed the 1822 revolt) as its first emperor. However, Canning's stabilisation of Portugal suffered a setback in 1826. King John died leaving Pedro as the heir to the throne. The liberal-minded Pedro drew up a charter for the continuation of parliamentary government but declined to return to Portugal. Instead he handed over the throne to his daughter Maria to reign as his regent/successor. Meanwhile, Pedro's brother Dom Miguel was still lurking in the background, and, with the support of the Spanish absolutists was looking for another opportunity to stage a coup. By late 1826 supporters of Miguel were gathering threateningly along the Spanish-Portugese border. Metternich summed up the feelings of the absolutists when he declared that Miguel was free to do anything he pleased and in November 1826 his supporters launched an invasion of northern Portugal with the clear aim of deposing Maria. Canning had hoped to avoid the necessity for direct British intervention, but the actions of the 'Miguelists' left him little choice. Public opinion was furious at the impending collapse of constitutionalism in Portugal and Treaty obligations really required Britain to come to the aid of the legitimate government. In December 5000 British troops were despatched to Portugal where their presence encouraged the Portugese army sufficiently to enable them to defeat Miguel's forces. For the time being Maria's succession to the throne seemed to have been secured and the liberal constitution saved. However, Miguel continued to claim the succession and the uneasy state of Portuguese affairs was still unresolved in 1827 when Canning died.

5 Canning and the Greek Question

For fuller details of Canning's handling of the question of Greek independence you should see Chapter 5 which deals specifically with the Eastern Question throughout the whole period 1815-65. However, at this point it is important to stress that Canning's approach to the ongoing Greek revolt reflected his general conviction that European problems needed to be dealt with as distinct issues rather than in the context of congresses developing principles for general application.

6 Comparing Castlereagh and Canning

For a full consideration of this debate you will need to read the appropriate section in Chapter 7 which deals with contrasts in approach to British foreign policy over the period 1815-65 as a whole and looks at the historiographical arguments which have arisen. At this point we need to focus on the evidence relating to specific aspects of policy, which needs to be discussed in response to what remains a very popular examination topic.

Castlereagh and Canning certainly came to have different attitudes towards the value of the Congress System. However, there is no evidence to suggest that Canning originally had severe criticisms of Castlereagh's policy at the Vienna Congress or of the terms of the Quadruple Alliance. Though out of office until 1816, Canning was willing to accept Liverpool's offer to go to Portugal as Ambassador in 1814 and he remained in that post until 1816, thus associating himself very directly with British foreign policy. Similarly, his earlier conflict with Castlereagh which resulted in the infamous duel of 1809 had nothing to do with foreign policy as such and the two men considered the matter closed in 1812 when Castlereagh offered to stand down from the Foreign Office in favour of Canning. Although Canning was not willing to accept the offer, he privately considered it a generous one on Castlereagh's part. We cannot therefore subscribe to the idea of personal differences or differences over the Peace Settlement as standing between them.

From 1816 to 1820 Canning sat in the Cabinet with Castlereagh, and again there is no evidence of any serious differences of opinion. On the contrary, it appears that Castlereagh was willing to consult Canning and there is evidence to suggest that the two men may have collaborated to some extent over the famous State Paper of 1820. Canning's resignation at the end of 1820 was over the Queen Caroline affair and came only after he had agonised for months over his position and done his best to avoid abandoning office. This hardly suggests that he was seriously at odds with the conduct of foreign policy. Furthermore all the discussions about Canning's return to office (which began almost as soon as he had left it) centred around his possible appointment as Home Secretary and possibly as Leader of the Commons. Castlereagh inherited his father's title as Marquess of Londonderry in 1820 and the possibility arose of that peerage being elevated to the rank of a full UK peerage with Castlereagh going to the House of Lords and retaining the Foreign Office. This would have left the leadership of the Commons open for Canning. All this reinforces the view that Canning saw nothing to object to in Castlereagh's handling of foreign policy but was mainly concerned with his own status and his wish not to accept anything less than first place in the House of Commons.

It seems fairly clear that Castlereagh and Canning were in general agreement about the nature of British interest in relation to issues such as Spain, Portugal, Latin America and Greece. Castlereagh wanted to avoid French or Allied intervention in Spain - so did Canning; Castlereagh saw Portugal as a sticking point over which war would have to be undertaken - so did Canning; Castlereagh wanted to detach the issue of Latin America from the Spanish Question - this was a central issue to Canning; Castlereagh sympathized with the Greeks whilst at the same time wanting to do nothing to undermine the basic integrity of Turkey-in-Europe - this was precisely Canning's reaction. However, there were basic differences in their methods and their ideas about how to achieve their aims in all these areas. Castlereagh based his approach on the idea that the Alliance which had defeated Napoleon could provide the mechanism for resolving disputes and problems. Canning saw Britain disengaging from continental affairs to the extent that it could become more of a spectator, occasionally entering the diplomatic game to provide a corrective to the direction of events, either gently or more forcibly as the case might require. However, it must be remembered that Castlereagh himself was far from happy with the way that congresses had worked out in practice. How much longer he would have persevered with them had he failed to realise his aims at Verona is simply speculation, but it is at least arguable that his policy in the rest of the 1820s, had he lived, might not have been much different from that of Canning.

Relations with Austria were an area of considerable divergence between the two men. Castlereagh saw Austria as a key element in the diplomatic balance of Europe and this goes a long way to explaining the emphasis he put on his relations with Metternich. Castlereagh's view of Austria was heavily influenced by the diplomatic world of the era before the French Wars and derived from Pitt's ideas about the European balance. Canning's relative detachment during the crucial years from 1809 to 1815 possibly enabled him to see Austria in a more realistic light. He seems to have accepted that Austria would find it impossible to pursue a policy which did not accommodate either Russia or France, that Austria would always need the support of one or other of the great powers. He saw Austria as in basically the same situation as Prussia which at that point did not really rank as a 'great power'. This did not mean that Canning was indifferent to the fate of

Austria - merely that he did not see that Britain could achieve anything particularly constructive through an Austrian connection. He did not know Metternich personally and he had no great regard for his abilities. In these respects, of course, he differed significantly from Castlereagh.

7 From Canning to Palmerston, 1827-30

As noted above, Canning succeeded Liverpool as Prime Minister in April 1827. It was a significant turning point in the political balance of the period. To begin with, Canning's elevation was resisted by George IV, just as his return to the Cabinet had been in 1822. In the end the King had to accept that Canning's prominence and the customary uncertain state of the House of Commons meant that there was no viable alternative Premier unless Canning was prepared to serve under another leader - this, at the age of 57, he was understandably not willing to do. However, Canning could not persuade those of his Tory colleagues who were still against the idea of Catholic Emancipation to continue in government with him because they assumed that a Canning-led ministry would bring forward Emancipation sooner or later. This meant that he lost several top Tories, including the Duke of Wellington and Robert Peel. In order to form a viable ministry Canning was compelled to turn to the Whigs, who agreed to enter a coalition. So far as foreign policy was concerned Canning was naturally determined to retain ultimate control. Apparently he intended to be Prime Minister and Foreign Secretary in the longer term, but difficulties in placing ministers appropriately and in conformity to their own wishes meant that he ended up having to act as his own Chancellor of the Exchequer. He therefore persuaded a personal friend, Lord Dudley, to go to the Foreign Office with the understanding (entirely approved of by Dudley) that Canning would tell him what to do.

The death of Canning in August 1827 threw the political world into even more confusion. Lord Goderich, a seasoned minister but hardly prime ministerial material, carried on the government for a few months but his heart was not really in it and by the end of the year he was virtually begging the King to find another Prime Minister. The King, who had never liked the idea of a government dominated by pro-Catholic elements, was only too happy to turn to the Duke of Wellington, who duly formed a ministry with Peel as Home Secretary and Leader of the Commons. Ironically it was this ministry which, in 1829, was forced by the deteriorating situation in Ireland to concede Catholic Emancipation.

The prestige and political significance of the Duke of Wellington is often ignored or at least marginalised by writers on the period. His influence in all areas of policy was immense. In 1819, he stabilised Liverpool's tottering government simply by agreeing to join the

Cabinet. In 1822 he had been the decisive factor in Canning's return when he advised the King not to resist his reappointment - the King having suggested that Wellington himself go to the Foreign Office. In fact Wellington only took office as Foreign Secretary on one occasion - 1834-5 during Peel's so-called '100 day administration'. However, his opinions on foreign policy were difficult to ignore even when (as was often the case with Canning) they were not particularly welcome. Wellington was generally what must be called a 'reactionary' in terms of foreign policy. He disliked popular or nationalistic movements and he had little sympathy with constitutionalists. He did not have much faith in his own countrymen's ability to run a political system any more democratic than that which they enjoyed already and he had no faith at all in the ability of foreign peoples. He tended instinctively to sympathise with the rights of sovereigns - even those with a despotic and tyrannical tendency. After 1822, he soon repented of his support for Canning's return to the Foreign Office and became a Cabinet critic of his policy. His opposition made life difficult for Canning at times and occasionally affected his decisions. For example, Canning would have recognised the South American colonies' claims to independence earlier had it not been for Wellington's opposition.

When Wellington became Prime Minister at the beginning of 1828, he appointed Lord Aberdeen as Foreign Secretary. Aberdeen had diplomatic experience going back to Castlereagh's time and had been the latter's diplomatic envoy to Britain's allies in 1813 during the final push against Napoleon. Initially Wellington seemed to have reunited the Tories since he was able to bring into his government most of the 'Canningite' Tories who had remained with Canning the previous year. These included William Huskisson, Viscount Palmerston and William Lamb (later Lord Melbourne) who, remarkably, as a pro-Catholic retained his post as Chief Secretary for Ireland. This unity however was short-lived. The Canningite Tories soon fell out with Wellington and Peel over the reallocation of parliamentary seats which had been freed when (as occasionally happened) a depopulated borough was disenfranchised. The Canningites resigned and Wellington was left heading a weakened 'Protestant' government. Wellington and Aberdeen pursued a rather different policy from that of Canning. On the Greek Question, Wellington proved pragmatic rather than principled. The Prime Minister and his Foreign Secretary did not quite see eye to eye over this issue but Wellington's dominance ensured that he had the last word. Initially hoping to appease and bolster the Turks, he ended up ruthlessly forcing the case for Greek independence. In Portugal he tolerated the virtual collapse of Canning's policy in 1828, when Dom Miguel launched a long-anticipated and successful *coup d'état* and proceeded to eliminate all vestiges of liberal constitutionalism with a policy of arbitrary arrests and executions. Wellington's government not only tolerated this, it even allowed Miguel to send a fleet to capture Madeira. This policy drove an even greater wedge between Wellington and the Canningites who saw their late master's careful policy reduced to a mockery. Wellington did not even react very strongly when Miguel's regime mistreated a British subject, an issue which drew robust condemnation from Palmerston who was rapidly emerging as the leading Canningite figure.

The policy pursued by Wellington and Aberdeen produced a clearer division over foreign policy in British politics. On one hand there were those who preferred to tolerate absolutism and repression in the supposed interests of stability and to deter revolution. On the other hand there were those who advanced the claims of constitutionalism and liberal attitudes as the best guarantees of stability and the avoidance of revolution. It was a division largely caused by Wellington's personal opinions. Although his views did command wider support (not least from the King), inside his own government both Peel and Aberdeen were rather more liberal in their opinions than their leader. When Wellington's government fell in November 1830, Lord Grey's new Whig-led coalition ministry, pledged primarily to deal with the major domestic issue of parliamentary reform, was also committed to a new direction in foreign policy.

Making notes on 'Castlereagh, Canning and the Maintenance of the European Settlement'

Your notes on the period 1815-30 should enable you to identify and understand the nature of the main problems which faced European diplomacy in the years immediately after the Vienna Settlement. You should have a clear idea of the Congress System and the reasons why it ultimately broke down. You should also be able to reach some conclusions about the differences between Castlereagh and Canning in their handling of foreign policy.

If you carry out the following tasks you should ensure you gain the understandings you require:

1. Summarise briefly what happened at each of the congresses held between 1818 and 1822.
2. Describe what issues were at stake for Britain in the case of:
a) Spain,
b) Italy,
c) Portugal,
d) Latin America, and
e) Greece.
3. Make a list of the ways in which Castlereagh and Canning agreed and differed in:
a) ideas,
b) aims, and
c) methods.

Answering essay questions on 'Castlereagh, Canning and the Maintenance of the European Settlement'.

The questions asked specifically on this period - as opposed to those placing it within some longer-term context - can generally be classified into three types:

a) those which ask for an assessment of Castlereagh (this would involve referring back to the Vienna Settlement itself, as well as the period up to 1822);

b) those which ask for an assessment of Canning;

c) those which invite a comparison between the two.

Examples of such questions, to which you might plan responses, are:

1. How successfully did Castlereagh secure and then protect British interests in his foreign policy 1815-22?

   Note that this is a two-part question with the keywords 'secure' and 'protect' requiring separate analysis - do not assume that the assessment will be the same in each case. Remember to use evaluative expressions such as 'very successful', 'not very successful', 'successful in some ways and not in others', etc.

2. To what extent was Castlereagh 'dazzled and deceived' by European leaders 1815-22?

   Another evaluative and two-part exercise. Note that 'dazzled' and 'deceived' are not the same thing. You may consider that one or other is justified or unjustified but not both - in any event you must discuss them separately.

3. Was the 'Congress System' a misconceived idea which was bound to end in failure from Britain's point of view?

   This involves a more direct judgement. You need to focus on 'misconceived' and define that expression precisely. The phrase 'bound to end in failure' carries with it an assumption of inevitability which needs to be discussed whether or not you agree with the idea.

4. How successful was Canning in pursuing Britain's national interests 1822-7?

   This is relatively straightforward as an evaluative question but remember to discuss what Britain's 'national interests' were or might be argued to be in this period as well as discussing how Canning handled particular issues.

5. Did the death of Castlereagh bring about any significant change in the direction of British foreign policy?

   This is the classic comparison essay (although Canning is not mentioned in the question) so remember to aim for some balance between the two elements (similarities and differences). The keywords for discussion are 'significant' and 'direction' - how you define these two words will set the course for your argument.

Source-based questions on 'Castlereagh, Canning and the Maintenance of the European Settlement'.

1. The Congress System

Read the extract from Castlereagh's modification of Article VI of the Quadruple Alliance, as explained to the Cabinet in 1818, on page 40.

a) How, according to this source, were the arrangements relating to the calling of congresses to be altered? (5 marks)

b) What, if any, reservations might Canning have had about these new arrangements and what aspects would have been likely to meet with his approval? (10 marks)

2. Britain and 'Interventionism'

Read the extract from the State Paper of May 1820 on page 41.

a) What exactly is meant by the expression 'the late policy of the King of Spain'? (5 marks)

b) In your own words, explain the reasons why Castlereagh is ruling out British agreement to intervention in Spain? (10 marks)

c) In what ways does the tone and language used by Castlereagh indicate that this was intended to be a firm and decisive statement of the British position? (10 marks)

3. Britain and the 'Troppau Protocol'

Read the extracts from the 'Protocol' on page 43.

a) In your own words explain what, according to Section 1, was to be the criterion for intervention in the affairs of particular countries. (10 marks)

b) Which area where revolts occurred in 1820-21 do you think best fitted the conditions for intervention by the allies, as specified in Section 1, and why? (10 marks)

c) How far do the ideas expressed in these three sections contradict the ideas set out in the State Paper of May 1820? (10 marks)

Summary Diagram
Castlereagh, Canning and the European Settlement, 1815-30

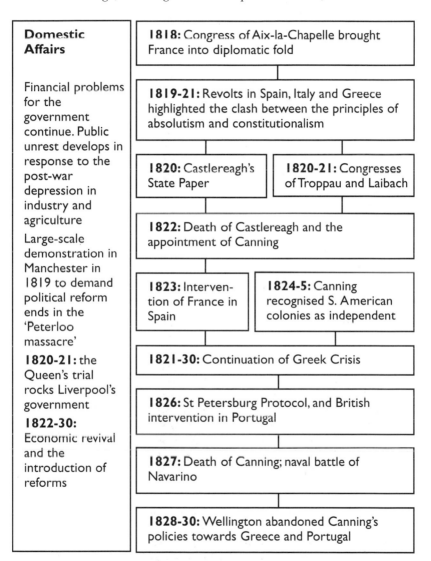

Domestic Affairs	
Financial problems for the government continue. Public unrest develops in response to the post-war depression in industry and agriculture	**1818:** Congress of Aix-la-Chapelle brought France into diplomatic fold
	1819-21: Revolts in Spain, Italy and Greece highlighted the clash between the principles of absolutism and constitutionalism
	1820: Castlereagh's State Paper — **1820-21:** Congresses of Troppau and Laibach

Domestic Affairs

Financial problems for the government continue. Public unrest develops in response to the post-war depression in industry and agriculture

Large-scale demonstration in Manchester in 1819 to demand political reform ends in the 'Peterloo massacre'

1820-21: the Queen's trial rocks Liverpool's government

1822-30: Economic revival and the introduction of reforms

1818: Congress of Aix-la-Chapelle brought France into diplomatic fold

1819-21: Revolts in Spain, Italy and Greece highlighted the clash between the principles of absolutism and constitutionalism

1820: Castlereagh's State Paper

1820-21: Congresses of Troppau and Laibach

1822: Death of Castlereagh and the appointment of Canning

1823: Intervention of France in Spain

1824-5: Canning recognised S. American colonies as independent

1821-30: Continuation of Greek Crisis

1826: St Petersburg Protocol, and British intervention in Portugal

1827: Death of Canning; naval battle of Navarino

1828-30: Wellington abandoned Canning's policies towards Greece and Portugal

4 Palmerston and the Changing Scene in Europe, 1830-51

The 1830s saw the start of the gradual erosion of the Vienna Settlement of 1815, which, in their different ways, both Castlereagh and Canning had tried to sustain in the 1820s. As with so much to do with foreign policy, it was largely events outside of Britain's direct control which brought about changes in Britain's perception of relations with the other European powers. At the start of the 1830s, British policy was still based primarily on the idea that the principal threat to the future peace and tranquillity of Europe lay in the resurgence of an aggressive and expansionist France. By the early 1850s it was Russia which was the principal object of suspicion and Britain was on the verge of an alliance with France against Russia and, moreover, a France in which a Bonaparte once again held the reins of power. Over most of this period the Foreign Office was dominated by one of the most controversial ministers ever to hold the post of Foreign Secretary - Lord Palmerston.

1 Henry John Temple, 3rd Viscount Palmerston (1784-1865)

Palmerston was born in London, the heir to an Irish peerage. His was not one of those Irish titles granted full UK status under the Act of Union of Great Britain and Ireland in 1800. He was therefore entitled to enter the House of Commons which he duly did in 1807. Unusually, he did so having already secured a junior government post at the Admiralty. In the next 58 years up to his death he was to spend only one short period of six months out of the Commons and indeed remarkably little time out of government office - 48 of those years were to be occupied in some kind of ministerial post, including a total of 16 years as Foreign Secretary and nearly 10 years as Prime Minister.

Palmerston's amazing record of holding on to office can partly be explained by his need for the salary which political office brought. Although he inherited a peerage and estates in Hampshire and Sligo on the west coast of Ireland, he also inherited the results of his father's financial incompetence and extravagance in the form of mortgages against his property which ate up a considerable amount of his annual revenues. Basically, Palmerston needed his political salary to boost his income - when out of office he tended to feel the pinch!

Palmerston entered politics as a Tory in the Portland administration of 1807-9. He continued serving under Spencer Percival and then Lord Liverpool at the unglamorous post of Secretary-at-War (not to be confused with the much more prestigious post of Secretary for War and Colonies). The Secretary-at-War was responsible for the financial and general administration of the army and it was not automatic for the holder to be given a place in the Cabinet. Although Palmerston was in fact offered Cabinet status by Percival in 1809, he turned it down on the grounds that he was too young and his office too lowly. As it turned out, this was a mistake, because subsequently Palmerston had to wait until 1827 and the formation of the Canning ministry before he was finally able to achieve the status of a Cabinet Minister.

Palmerston's acceptance of a post in Canning's government marked the conclusion of a gradual process, starting in 1822, by which Palmerston had drawn closer politically to Canning. He agreed with Canning over the critical issue of Catholic Emancipation and whilst he had not been particularly close to him in his early years in politics, he had always admired Canning's abilities. Incidentally, this admiration was not mutual - Canning seems to have regarded Palmerston as a man of limited ability. Palmerston's emergence as a Canningite left him estranged from the more orthodox Tories and, although he remained in office with Wellington at the start of the latter's ministry of 1828, he soon fell out with the Prime Minister and resigned along with the other Canningites. It was to be his first experience of being out of office since entering Parliament, and over the next couple of years he became increasingly critical of his former colleagues. This was particularly so over foreign policy issues such as Greece and Portugal, where he believed Wellington's clumsy and narrow-minded approach was wrecking the careful policies of Canning.

When Wellington's government fell at the end of 1830 over the issue of Wellington's absolute refusal to contemplate any concessions over the reform of the electoral system, it was clear that only Lord Grey, the Whig leader who was committed to some kind of parliamentary reform, was in a position to form a new ministry. It was equally clear that Grey could not do this on the basis of a purely Whig government since there were insufficient Whigs with suitable experience - such a government could not have hoped to command support in the House of Commons. This meant that Grey had to form a coalition and that the Canningites, who were now prepared to accept the need for parliamentary reform, were strongly placed to obtain high offices. Although Palmerston was therefore virtually certain to figure in the new Cabinet, it was a surprise to most people when he was made Foreign Secretary. Grey originally offered the post to Lord Lansdowne, who declined it and suggested Palmerston instead. The appointment attracted little general enthusiasm, and the idea that Palmerston would become one of the great foreign secretaries probably occurred to nobody except perhaps Palmerston himself and his former mistress Princess Lieven, the wife of the Russian Ambassador, who had championed his elevation to the post and who, quite undeservedly, subsequently claimed the credit for getting him the job!

2 The Belgian Crisis

Two major international crises occurred early in Palmerston's years at the Foreign Office to test the calibre of the new Foreign Secretary. One was related to the Eastern Question and is dealt with in Chapter 5, the other was closer to home in that sensitive area for British interests, the Low Countries.

In 1815 the union of Belgium with Holland had seemed to be a sensible decision from many points of view. Belgium had previously been part of the Austrian Empire known as the Austrian Netherlands and had no tradition of independent status. The economies of Belgium and Holland seemed to complement each other well. Holland had a strong maritime trade and imperial possessions as well as an established monarchy and political structure - Belgium had a mixed agricultural and industrial base. Together, the two seemed to offer a stabilising counterpoise to any future expansionism on the part of France. These factors seemed to outweigh the obvious differences of religion and language which existed - Belgium was Catholic and mainly French-speaking, while the people of Holland were Protestant and of course spoke Dutch. From the British point of view, in particular, these differences seemed to be of secondary importance to the overall strategic and economic advantages of the union. Britain after all was a state made up of Protestants and Catholics and in which the state church in Scotland was Presbyterian as opposed to Anglican in England, Wales and Ireland. Catholics were the overwhelming majority in Ireland whilst nonconformity was rapidly becoming predominant in Wales. Despite the increasing dominance of the English language, there were still many parts of Wales where English was hardly spoken or understood, and the same was true in Ireland and Scotland. Therefore it was not entirely surprising that, given the priorities of 1815, Castlereagh had not considered the union of Belgium and Holland to be controversial.

Had the Dutch behaved more reasonably there is every chance that the experiment would have succeeded. However, after 1815 the resentment of Belgians at their status within the union and with the policies pursued by the joint government grew. Finally, these tensions resulted in a full-scale revolt in August 1830.

a) The Causes of Belgian Resentment

Basically the religious, cultural and linguistic differences between the Belgians and Dutch were exacerbated by Belgian economic and political grievances. The Dutch agricultural and commercial interests favoured a policy of free trade, with minimum restrictions on imports and exports and low tariffs. The Belgians increasingly favoured a protective system of tariffs which they felt would benefit their developing industrial sector. Politically, the Dutch monopolised the offices of government and this ensured that their interests and language took precedence. In the joint parliament Belgian and Dutch representation was equal, despite the fact that the Belgian population was almost twice as large. Also the Dutch-dominated government was too illiberal in its politics for Belgian taste - press restrictions were a particular objectionable aspect of this.

b) The Revolt and its Consequences

The Belgians rebelled against the union in August 1830 and in October declared themselves independent. They announced their separation from the Dutch crown and declared their intention to set up their own hereditary monarchy. This was a challenge to the Vienna Settlement and the situation was made worse when the Belgians chose to elect as their new King the Duke of Nemours who was a younger son of the French King, Louis-Philippe. This choice reflected the fact that most Belgians looked to France as their main hope for the future. Many in Belgium hoped that sooner or later they would be able to unite with France. For precisely that reason such an obvious French connection was out of the question as far as Britain was concerned. When Louis-Philippe himself ruled his son out of consideration it was under pressure from the British government. Palmerston at first suggested that the Belgians be ruled by the eldest son of the Dutch King, who was known to be far more liberal than his father. This of course was totally unacceptable to the Belgians since the two countries would eventually have ended up under the same crown - i.e. independence in name only. In June 1831, the Belgians opted for the much less controversial Prince Leopold of Saxe-Coburg who was an acceptable compromise to both Britain and France. Leopold had the good fortune to be related to the British royal family and to be about to marry the daughter of Louis-Philippe. However, the Dutch tried to resist the Belgian declaration of independence by force and Britain and France eventually had to intervene to compel the Dutch to accept a ceasefire in 1833. It was not until 1839 that a full final settlement (the Treaty of London) was reached. That settlement contained a guarantee of respect for the future neutrality of Belgium, which was accepted by all the major powers, and it was the violation of that guarantee by Germany in 1914 which eventually provided the justification for British entry into the First World War.

c) Palmerston's Handling of the Belgian Crisis

As can be seen from the above outline of events, the initial developments of the crisis had already occurred by the time Palmerston became Foreign Secretary in November 1830. The situation had all the ingredients to test British attitudes to intervention. This was a rebellion against a sovereign whose authority to rule was established under the Vienna Settlement. On the other hand, the actions of that sovereign seemed to justify the Belgians' claim that they had been misgoverned under the union. To add to this was the fact that the region affected was one of direct and central importance to British interests - it was, after all, French expansion into the Low Countries which had been the original cause of outbreak of the French Wars in 1793. British interests therefore dictated that whatever settlement was reached over Belgium should not involve any extension of French influence and should be based on terms which could be sustained for the foreseeable future.

Palmerston was clear in his own mind from the outset that the only long-term solution to the crisis was for Belgium to become an independent country with generally recognised neutral status. Shortly after taking office he sent the following information to the British representative in Brussels:

1 His Majesty's Government considers the absolute and entire separation of Belgium from Holland to be no longer a matter for discussion, but to have become, by the course of events, as established, and as far as can at present be foreseen, an irreversible fact.

This was not the result of any personal sympathy for the Belgians on Palmerston's part - on the contrary, he would have much preferred to see the 1815 union maintained, as he explained to the Prussians at the end of December 1830:

1 It was for the interest of both England and Prussia that Belgium and Holland should have remained united, if their union could have been maintained; but that union having become impossible by the force of events, it is obvious that the independence of Belgium is the only means
5 of preventing another union which would be in the highest degree objectionable to Prussia and England, and which could not even be attempted without involving Europe in war.

When Palmerston referred to 'another union' he meant, of course, a union between Belgium and France. Such an outcome was totally unacceptable. Palmerston was not prepared to allow even the semblance of Belgian dependence on France, much less a union which, to all practical intents, would be an enlargement of French territory through the annexation of Belgium.

Palmerston was assisted in bringing the Belgian crisis to a conclusion which was satisfactory from the British point of view by a number of factors:

(i) The new French King, Louis-Philippe, having just secured his crown through a revolution which had ousted the Bourbons, needed to consolidate his position in France - the last thing he needed was a war against Britain, which was almost certain to bring the Prussians in against France as well.

(ii) The blame for the crisis could be fixed on the Dutch King. Palmerston believed that, had it not been for William I's stupidity and intransigence, the grievances of the Belgians would never have escalated into rebellion in the first place. He was therefore prepared to force William to accept a settlement giving the Belgians independence if that was necessary.

(iii) Palmerston was left a virtually free hand by Russia and Austria in this crisis. The Russians were distracted by a serious revolt in Poland which absorbed their attention; the Austrians were diverted by revolts in a number of Italian states. These outbreaks occurred in the first few weeks after Palmerston took office.

Initially therefore, Palmerston had no difficulty in getting general diplomatic agreement with the great powers for the principle of Belgian independence. He began with true Canning methodology by working with the principal object of his suspicion, the French. Britain and France together sponsored the cause of the Belgians, just as Britain and Russia in 1826-7 had advocated the cause of the Greeks. A hitch nearly arose over the Belgians' choice of Louis-Philippe's son as their new King, but this was resolved by the compromise candidate, Leopold of Saxe-Coburg, being generally accepted. However, things were then made much worse when the Dutch sent troops into Belgium in August 1831 to restore their authority - a move which forced the French to send in their own troops to support the Belgians since public opinion in France left Louis-Philippe little choice but to act.

This was nearly a disaster for Palmerston. His only realistic option was to threaten the French with war if they did not withdraw - fortunately Louis-Philippe feared the consequences of a war even more than he feared French public opinion, and French troops were withdrawn. Palmerston still faced the problem of forcing the Dutch to face up to the reality of Belgian independence. A treaty giving Belgium independence under Leopold was drawn up in November 1831 and agreed by the major powers, but the Dutch refused to accept it or to concede the areas allocated to Belgium, which included the commercial centre of Antwerp. In 1832 Palmerston finally forced a conclusion to the stalemate by allying with the French to force the Dutch out. British and French naval forces blockaded the Dutch coast, whilst the French army, this time with Palmerston's support, marched on Antwerp and forced the Dutch to give up that key port. The blockade eventually started hitting Dutch business interests and by May 1833 the Dutch government agreed to accept the treaty of November 1831, although, as stated above, the finer points of the settlement were not finalised to Palmerston's satisfaction until the Treaty of London of 1839.

The Belgian crisis highlights the difficulties which faced Palmerston and, for that matter, those confronting any British foreign secretary. He was criticised on all sides for his handling of the situation. The radicals criticised him because they were pro-Belgian and pro-French and opposed Palmerston's refusal to allow the Belgians their first choice as ruler, the Duke of Nemours. They later criticised his threat of war in 1831. The Tories complained that Palmerston was supporting revolution and ignoring the legitimate authority of the Dutch King. They were incensed by the joint action with France in 1832. William IV (1830-37) also disliked Palmerston's policy. He detested the French, having fought as a naval officer against them in two wars, and his opposition forced Palmerston to limit British action in 1832 to joint participation in the blockade, rather than joint military intervention with the French army.

3 Palmerston and Russia: Cooperation and Suspicion

As was pointed out in Chapter 1, relations between Britain and Russia had been increasingly complex since the latter's emergence as a force in international affairs during the second half of the eighteenth century. Both Castlereagh and Canning had recognised the need to keep a check on Russia's expansionist tendencies. Castlereagh had attempted to do this by involving Tsar Alexander I in the Quadruple Alliance and a system of collective agreements; Canning had favoured working directly with Russia to reach bilateral understandings. This was an approach which was rendered more straightforward by the death of the unpredictable Alexander in 1826 and his replacement by his more stable and down-to-earth brother, Nicholas I. Palmerston definitely preferred Canning's approach. He was, in general terms, pro-Russian in attitude in the years before he became Foreign Secretary and enjoyed an intimate friendship with the long-serving Russian Ambassador to London, Count Lieven, as well as an intimate relationship with the Ambassador's wife. In these early years, and even during his first two periods at the Foreign Office, Palmerston showed little sympathy with those radicals and liberal-minded Whigs who routinely condemned Russian autocracy and oppression. The great liberal cause in relation to Russia was the Polish Question. Russia had overseen the partitions of the old Polish kingdom in the 1790s and had annexed the greater part of it into the Russian Empire. Emigré Poles, exiled from their homeland, were concentrated in Paris and London and they kept up a pressure, which by Palmerston's time was into a second generation, on French and British governments to secure the freedom of their country from what they described as Russian tyranny.

As Foreign Secretary, Palmerston did his best to avoid the attention of those Polish exiles in London and their radical supporters who constantly pressed their attentions on the Foreign Office. He regularly found excuses not to meet with deputations which attempted to foist petitions on him. During the Polish revolt of 1831, he declined in very strong terms to receive a petition in support of the rebels from the Westminster Political Union. He also did his best to persuade the French government not to help the Poles. In the summer of 1831, the veteran French statesman Talleyrand proposed that Britain and France should make a joint offer to mediate between the Poles and the Russians - Palmerston would have none of this. He ruled out any question of aid in any form and held steadfastly to the view that this was an internal Russian matter and that Britain should not intrude. He summed up his position in terms of sheer expediency:

| the English nation is able to make war, but it will only do so where its own interests are concerned. We are a simple and practical nation, a commercial nation; we do not fight for others as the French do.

Palmerston was equally uninterested in the claims of the liberals in Spain. The brutal rule of King Ferdinand VII was causing outrage amongst liberals all over Europe and particularly in Britain and France. As with Poland, Palmerston urged the French not to intervene and he took no action other than a formal protest when the Spanish government executed two British subjects accused of involvement with the revolutionary guerrilla movement. King Ferdinand died in 1833 leaving a disputed succession between absolutist and liberal factions which resulted in civil war over the next few years. In Portugal Palmerston did give diplomatic support to King Pedro in 1832, when the liberal monarch returned to oust his younger brother Miguel who had usurped the throne in 1828. However no actual intervention was made and the most Palmerston would do was to ignore the involvement of British volunteers on Pedro's side - which was strictly speaking illegal under British law. This generally conservative attitude, virtually 'Wellingtonian' to all practical purposes, made Palmerston seem an unlikely claimant to Canningite principles and convinced Metternich that a Whig-led government in London might not be the terrible thing he had feared.

Palmerston's pro-Russianism received a severe shock when news of the Treaty of Unkiar Skelessi, terminating the conflict between Russia and Turkey, broke in 1833 (see pages 87-106 for a detailed consideration of Palmerston's handling of the Eastern Question in this period). During the conflict Palmerston had been at pains to defend and explain the Russian position, and the realisation that Russia had now imposed a treaty which was clearly contrary to British interests left him embarrassed and angry. His feelings towards the Russians were never quite the same after this, although it would be going too far to suggest that he switched to an anti-Russian posture immediately. Nevertheless in 1834 he developed the idea of a Quadruple Alliance of Great Britain, France, Spain and Portugal (which by then both had liberal monarchies) to counterbalance the Holy Alliance powers of Eastern Europe. Unkiar Skelessi had the effect of ensuring that Palmerston would spend the rest of the 1830s looking for an opportunity to drive back Russian influence from Turkey. When it came, in the form of the second Mehemet Ali crisis in 1839, Palmerston used Canningite methods to avoid a direct confrontation with Russia, but nevertheless was able to ensure that the damage done to British interests by the 1833 treaty was reversed.

When Palmerston left office in 1841 to be replaced by Lord Aberdeen he had good reason to feel that, with the signing of the Straits Convention (see page 94-5), Anglo-Russian relations were back on a stable basis. As explained on page 95, the only really significant Anglo-Russian development of note during the Peel administration's period of office from 1841 to 1846 was the visit of the Russian Tsar to London in 1844, during which his conversations with Peel and Aberdeen led him to that mistaken belief in the existence of an agreement with Britain over the future of Turkey which so fatally confused Anglo-Russian relations in the period before the outbreak of the Crimean War in 1854.

When Palmerston returned to the Foreign Office in 1846, Russia was not very prominent on the agenda of foreign policy. During the Conservatives' period of office, Aberdeen had brought about friendlier relations with France and there was some concern about whether Palmerston might ruin this since he was considered to be anti-French. However, the most decisive development came over events in Portugal, where a revolution broke out late in 1846. Although Palmerston favoured a neutral stance, he was forced by an odd turn of events into appearing to favour the rebels. In order to help resolve the crisis quickly, Palmerston initiated joint action with France and Spain to assist the Portuguese Queen to quell the revolt. At first this action brought strong criticism of him in the Commons from the radicals, but Palmerston was able to turn the situation to his advantage. The intervention which he had arranged included guarantees of an amnesty for the rebels and a return to constitutional government. Palmerston therefore argued that he had been acting in defence of constitutional principles and in order to protect the rebels from the brutal treatment which they might otherwise have suffered. The widespread acceptance of this explanation left Palmerston in the rather unlikely role of hero of the radicals. The support of the radicals in the Commons added to Palmerston's political strength and he began to enjoy his new status as well as to appreciate its political benefits. However, this was a stance which was not very compatible with a pro-Russian position since his new supporters detested the Russians with unrelenting fervour.

The outbreak of revolutions against absolutist or, in some cases, constitutional monarchs in Europe in 1848 (see page 72) sealed Palmerston's new image as the champion of European radicals.

British public opinion reacted angrily to the brutal suppression of revolts in Poland and Hungary by the Russians and Austrians. Palmerston, despite his private doubts about the destabilising effects of some of these outbreaks, was nevertheless propelled into a public association with the rebels (see page 73). By the time he was forced to leave the Foreign Office at the end of 1851 (see Section 7 of this chapter), he was firmly established in the mind of the public as a strong advocate of a tough policy towards Russia. When he returned to office in November 1852, this time as Home Secretary in a Whig-Peelite coalition government headed by Lord Aberdeen, Britain was already becoming locked into a trend of anti-Russianism which was to contribute to the eventual outbreak of the Crimean War in 1854 and Palmerston's own elevation to the premiership the following year.

4 Palmerston and France: Suspicion and Rapprochement

The attitudes of British politicians towards France in the early years following the Vienna Settlement were, not unnaturally, shaped by their feelings about the French Revolution and the subsequent French Wars. The Tories, initially inheriting the political dominance bequeathed to them by the great Pitt, saw the French Revolution as a catastrophe which had nearly brought European civilisation itself to an end. According to this point of view, the Revolution had not only spawned the destructive military despotism of Napoleon Bonaparte, but had also encouraged those radical and socialistic doctrines which now remained to threaten civilised society in the shape of demands for democratic political reform and social and economic equality. The Whigs, taking their political descent from Pitt's great rival, Charles James Fox, offered a rather different interpretation. According to their view the French Revolution had offered the benefits of individual freedom and sound representative government, but had been diverted from its true course by the opposition of the autocrats of Europe and British hostility resulting from the unfounded fears of Pitt's government. Because of this the Revolution had, as the Whigs saw it, become extreme and uncontrollable and had ended in the Bonapartist dictatorship. Therefore the Tories tended to see France as the repository of revolutionary ideas and influences tinged with a tendency towards militaristic expansionism, while the Whigs, on the other hand, tended to see France as the European leader of civilised and enlightened ideas.

Castlereagh, Canning, Peel, Wellington, Aberdeen and of course Palmerston were all men of the generation which had had to fight against Bonaparte and they were all, originally at least, Tories. These men were the dominant figures in British foreign policy from 1815 right through to 1865 when Palmerston's death brought to an end the political pre-eminence of the war generation. It is hardly surprising, therefore, that anti-French feelings, or at least a suspicious attitude towards France, was a consistent feature in British foreign policy. Palmerston's suspicions of France were strong enough for him to threaten war at one stage of the Belgian crisis and his policy during the second Mehemet Ali crisis of 1839-41, although primarily aimed at undoing the Treaty of Unkiar Skelessi, ended up with a strategy of isolating the French and cooperating with the Russians (see page 93). Palmerston's suspicious attitude towards France was not appreciated by many of his new Whig colleagues who held to the view that Britain and France as the Liberal-minded powers of Europe were natural allies. Many Whigs were opposed to Palmerston's policy of supporting the Sultan of Turkey in the 1839-41 crisis because they saw Mehemet Ali as an enlightened reformer who should be allowed to displace the Sultan and the corrupt Turkish regime and usher in a new era of efficient and progressive government for the Turkish Empire. To Palmerston, Mehemet Ali was nothing more than a French puppet whose increasing power represented a threat to British interests.

Palmerston continued to hold this basically anti-French attitude during the period 1841-6 when Peel's government was in power. He criticised the government's friendlier policy towards France which was developed by Peel and Aberdeen in 1842 and kept up a steady critical commentary until 1846 when Peel resigned. During this period control of foreign policy lay as much with Peel as with Aberdeen - possibly more so. Aberdeen was a reluctant Foreign Secretary in 1841 and almost throughout the whole period of the administration he seemed constantly to be on the verge of resigning, complaining about his health and the strains of office. He certainly did not enjoy (or want) the same degree of freedom which Palmerston was accustomed to exercise as Foreign Secretary. Peel kept up an almost incessant stream of correspondence with Aberdeen on foreign affairs and scrutinised every level of activity. He read, criticised and amended draft despatches and instructions; he suggested new points for consideration and even involved himself in diplomatic appointments. The degree of attention he gave to foreign policy was immense and it is probably more accurate to refer to Peel's foreign policy in this period than to that of Aberdeen. So far as France was concerned, Aberdeen's instincts were towards conciliation and closer relations. Peel, though he approved in general terms of Aberdeen's ideas, held this open-handed approach in firm check. Aberdeen was inclined towards an optimistic and conciliatory style in foreign policy. He was always ready to explain openly his intentions and to rely on the goodwill of the other side. Peel was less trusting, less optimistic and more inclined to play his cards close to his chest and use whatever means were available to reach his objectives. In his dealings with France, therefore, Peel made sure that Britain moved cautiously in the direction of closer relations.

Relations with France were complicated in this period by the question of the future of the Spanish monarchy - an issue which has become known as 'the Spanish Marriages'. Rival factions in Spain had taken the country into civil war during the 1830s and their endless plots and intrigues finally reached an uneasy tranquillity in 1843 when Queen Isabella was declared at the age of thirteen to be old enough to rule without a regent. The heir to the throne, for so long as Isabella remained unmarried and childless, was her younger sister Infanta [Princess] Louisa Fernanda. In this situation the question of the marriages of the Spanish princesses assumed an international political importance for future diplomatic and dynastic alliances. The British position was that the issue was one for the Spanish to decide provided that one main British condition was met - that there should be no marriage to members of the French Royal Family. British preference was for the Saxe-Coburg princes who were relatives of the British Prince Consort. Initially Aberdeen reached an agreement with the French Minister, Guizot, that it would be best to exclude both French and British connections from the marriages. By 1845 he had modified this position to the extent of indicating that Britain would not object to a French partner for Infanta Louisa Fernanda once Isabella was acceptably married and had produced heirs to the throne.

Palmerston's return to the Foreign Office in 1846 was initially seen as indicating a probable reversal in policy towards France. However, in the event, this did not happen. Palmerston's attitude was changed, partly because he knew that pro-French feeling amongst the Whigs was strong and partly because he subsequently approved of the new French government which emerged from the 1848 Revolution. Also Palmerston rather enjoyed his new-found popularity with the radicals, which was bound up with issues in which Russia appeared more and more as the threat, whilst France was cast more and more in the role of a potential ally. This transition surprised Palmerston himself, but by 1851 2, when he was engaged in what was in effect a struggle for his political future with Russell and the Crown, he could not afford to lose the political strength which his unlikely role as the radicals' hero had given him.

Over the question of the Spanish Marriages, however, Palmerston's relations with France got off to a shaky start. He apparently failed to grasp properly, or chose to disregard, the understanding which Aberdeen had reached with Guizot and offended the French by circulating proposals for the marriage of Isabella which included the Saxe-Coburg Prince Leopold, a cousin of Prince Albert, the Prince Consort, as a possible candidate. The French retaliated by sponsoring the marriage of Isabella to her cousin, the Duke of Cadiz, followed almost at once by the marriage of her sister, Louisa Fernanda, to a younger son of King Louis-Philippe. This alliance of the existing heir to the Spanish throne to a French prince left Britain in isolated protest and relations between London and Paris took on a distinctly icy tone. In the longer run the affair came to nothing since Isabella quickly produced children and thus made the prospect of a link between the Spanish and French thrones remote. In any case, by 1848 there was no French throne since Louis-Philippe was overthrown and a French Republic instituted.

As Britain moved tentatively towards a better relationship with the French a new pattern of future relations began to emerge. The roots of suspicion between Britain and France were never wholly removed. Cooperation became a matter of convenience or lack of options. For the rest of the nineteenth century and into the next, Anglo-French relations tended to veer between love and hate, cooperation and suspicion. Alliances were often reluctant and acrimonious and the threat of war sometimes hung heavy between the two countries. Even so, in the last analysis, from the Crimean War, in any conflicts in which both Britain and France have taken part, they have invariably been on the same side even if not always with any great enthusiasm!

5 The 1848 Revolutions

In 1848 a series of revolutions disturbed the general stability of Europe. France, the German states, the Austrian Empire and the Italian states were all affected. The movements behind these revolts were liberal and nationalistic in intent. There were strong social and economic factors also at work and socialist ideas also played a part in the unrest. Rapid industrialisation and the rise of the factory system had led to population shifts and the development of urban working-class communities which resented the appalling living and working conditions from which they suffered. Agricultural distress was also great in many areas of Europe in the 1840s. This mainly resulted from the potato blight (which had its most horrendous impact in Ireland where it resulted in around a million deaths), and poor corn harvest which sent food prices soaring beyond the reach of the poorer classes. Hunger drove people to violent demonstrations in France, the Rhineland and northern Italy. As is often the case with food short-ages, the distress was accompanied by the outbreak of epidemic diseases such as typhoid and cholera.

The distress of the lower classes coincided with increasing discon-tent among the middle classes who were increasingly demanding civil and political rights. In some cases this meant actually acquiring such rights because they had none at all; in others it meant adding to a limited range of rights which left them well short of being able to exercise any genuine political influence. In both types of case the target of their attack was the autocratic or semi-autocratic rulers and the ruling aristocracies which controlled the political, social and economic systems under which they lived. Apart from the revolution in France, all these risings eventually failed. In France the revolt led to a republic which by 1852 had been converted into a new Bonapartist Empire under Louis-Napoleon who became known as Napoleon III. Elsewhere the old regimes were quickly restored, although in the Italian state of Piedmont a liberal constitutional monarchy emerged and in the Austrian Empire serfdom was abolished.

The popular reaction in Britain to these revolutions was highly supportive. The massive public acclaim enjoyed by Palmerston in the late 1840s and the 1850s largely resulted from the perception of him in the public mind as the champion of the people and the scourge of autocrats. The reality was somewhat different. Privately Palmerston had many misgivings about the revolts and their likely effects. He was, after all, a conservative at heart. He was opposed to further parliamentary reform in Britain and, although he agreed with the idea that wider political rights were needed in the European countries, some of the more extreme democratic ideas which rose to the surface in 1848 went well beyond anything with which he could sympathise. He was particularly concerned about the fate of Austria because he saw the Austrian Empire as a stabilising factor in central Europe and he feared the consequences if the Empire crumbled - the obvious beneficiary would be Russia. Therefore, in many ways Palmerston was not sorry to see the demise of most of the 1848 revolts and the restoration of the old regimes, though he could not afford to say this in public. The most obvious immediate result from the British point of view was the overt hostility towards Russia and Austria which built up in the British public and press as a consequence of the brutality with which their armed forces suppressed the revolutionaries.

6 The 'Don Pacifico Debate' - 1850

In this section we will look, primarily through documentary extracts, at one of the most famous parliamentary debates of the nineteenth century. It has become known as the 'Don Pacifico debate'. The immediate cause of the debate was a motion from a radical MP, J.A. Roebuck, supporting Palmerston's conduct of foreign policy. Palmerston was coming under increasing criticism for his decision to support the claim of one David Pacifico for compensation from the Greek government following losses he sustained to his property in Athens during anti-Jewish riots in 1847. Don Pacifico was a Jewish businessman who had been born in Gibraltar and was therefore a British subject. From early childhood he had lived in Portugal and had become a naturalised Portuguese subject. He originally went to Athens as the Portuguese Consul but was dismissed for an attempted fraud against the Portuguese government. When he had first arrived in Athens he had used his Gibraltarian origin to secure a British passport and, with this security, he decided to remain in Athens after his dismissal. When his property was attacked, Pacifico applied to the British for help, and it was the failure of lengthy attempts to secure redress for him which led Palmerston in the end to sanction a blockade. In fact, Pacifico's case was only one of a number of strains between Britain and Greece which led to this action and the criticism of Palmerston stemmed from more than just his championing of Pacifico. It was rather the result of controversy about his handling of foreign policy over many years which came to a head with this particular issue. The debate raised again the whole question of British intervention in the affairs of other nations. It also raised issues of morality, the true nature of British interests and of Palmerston's fitness to conduct British foreign policy.

The motion, which was put forward in the House of Commons, was:

1 That the principles on which the Foreign Policy of Her Majesty's Government has been regulated, have been such as were calculated to maintain the honour and dignity of this country; and, in times of unexampled difficulty, to preserve peace between England and the nations of
5 the world.

Palmerston offered a review and a defence of his policies going back over twenty years. He referred in turn to his handling of affairs affecting Belgium, Portugal, Spain and Italy; he examined relations with the great powers and considered the questions of constitutionalism and the rights of British subjects abroad. He spoke for over four and a half hours with the aid of only a single sheet of brief notes. On the subject of Belgium, he had this to say:

1 (Document A) The people of Belgium evidently could not coalesce; and if certain Powers of Europe had combined at that moment to compel a reunion between these separate portions of the Kingdom of the Netherlands, I doubt whether that reunion could have been effected
5 without the immediate explosion of a war in Europe of the greatest magnitude; and I am quite sure that if it had been effected, it could not have lasted, and the foundation must have been laid thereby of future and inevitable disturbance. We carried out our opinion upon that point to a practical result ... Why, if ever there was an experiment - call it so
10 if you will - that fully and completely succeeded, the creation of Belgium into an independent State was that experiment.

He concluded:

1 I believe that the principles on which we have acted are those which are held by the great mass of the people of this country. I am convinced that these principles are calculated, so as the influence of England may properly be exercised with respect to the destinies of other countries, to
5 conduce to the maintenance of peace, to the advancement of civilisation, to the welfare and happiness of mankind ... It is a noble thing to be allowed to guide the policy and to influence the destinies of such a country ... while we have seen ... the political earthquake rolling Europe form side to side - while we have seen thrones shaken, shat-

10 tered, levelled; institutions overthrown and destroyed - while in almost
    every country of Europe the conflict of civil war has deluged the land
    with blood, from the Atlantic to the Black Sea, from the Baltic to the
    Mediterranean; this country has presented a spectacle honourable to
15 the people of England, and worthy of the admiration of mankind ... I
    contend that we have not in our foreign policy done anything to forfeit
    the confidence of the country ... I therefore fearlessly challenge the
    verdict which this House, as representing a political, a commercial, a
    constitutional country is to give on the question now brought before it;
20 where the principles on which the foreign policy of Her Majesty's
    Government has been conducted, and the sense of duty which led us to
    think ourselves bound to afford protection to our fellow subjects
    abroad, are proper and fitting guides for those who are charged with the
    Government of England; and whether, as the Roman, in days of old, held
25 himself free from indignity when he could say 'civis Romanus sum'; so
    also a British subject, in whatever land he may be, shall feel confident
    that the watchful eye and the strong arm of England, will protect him
    against injustice and wrong.

Gladstone, who at this time was emerging as a leading political figure,
and who detested both Palmerston's conduct of policy and his sexual
immorality responded:

1 (Document B) ... I will grapple with the noble Lord on the ground
   which he selected for himself ... that under his administration an
   Englishman should be, throughout the world, what the citizen of Rome
   had been. What then, Sir, was a Roman citizen? He was a member of a
5 privileged caste; he belonged to a conquering race, to a nation that held
   all others bound by the strong arm of power. For him there was to be an
   exceptional system of law; for him principles were to be asserted, and by
   him rights were to be enjoyed, that were denied to the rest of the
   world. Is such, then, the view of the noble Lord, as to the relation that is
10 to subsist between England and other countries ...? No, Sir, let it not be
   so; let us recognise, and recognise with frankness, the equality of the
   weak with the strong; the principles of brotherhood among nations, and
   of their sacred independence ... Let us refrain from all gratuitous and
   arbitrary meddling in the internal concerns of other States, even as we
15 should resent the same interference if it were attempted to be prac-
   tised towards ourselves.

Sir Robert Peel, who was, as it turned out, making the last speech of
his illustrious career, (he was to suffer a fatal riding accident the next
day) made the following contribution:

1 (Document C) The principle for which I contend ... is the principle for
   which every statesman of importance in this country for the last fifty
   years had contended - namely, non-interference with the domestic
   affairs of other countries, without some clear and unavoidable necessity

5 arising from circumstances affecting the interests of our own country
... Then, what are we to declare? That we will relinquish the principle of
non-interference, and declare in favour of the principle of self-government ...? If you do claim that right you must give a correlative right to
10 other powers ... who shall construe what is the basis of self-government? ... Recollect our manifold relations with other countries in every
corner of the globe. Recollect our position in North America. Recollect
our monarchical colonies, in close contact with republicanism ... Does
self-government extend beyond Europe? ... We govern millions of peo-
15 ple in India; are we to admit the right of other powers to inculcate the
right of self-government among them? Which is the wisest policy - to
attempt to interfere with the institutions and measures of the countries
not bordering on our own, out of an abstract love for constitutional
government - or to hold that doctrine maintained by Mr Fox, Mr Pitt,
20 Mr Canning and Lord Castlereagh, that the true policy of this country is
non-interference in the affairs of others ... It is also my firm belief that
you will not advance the cause of constitutional government by
attempting to dictate to other nations ... Constitutional liberty will
be best worked out by those who aspire to freedom by their own
25 efforts ...

The motion was carried by 310 votes to 264, a triumph for Palmerston
in parliamentary terms, while in the country at large support for his
approach to foreign affairs was immense. Most of his critics came
from his own class and from the intellectual elite. The middle-class
industrialists and the urban working classes were generally united in
their support for him. All the radicals in the House of Commons bar
one voted for him as did the small group of Chartist MPs. The country
squires and parsons, the professional classes of doctors and lawyers,
the commercial men of the City of London, and virtually the whole of
the Jewish community were all united in seeing Palmerston as their
spokesman when it came to the conduct of foreign affairs. Few politicians have ever achieved the breadth of support which Palmerston
received at this point in his career - seldom in the nineteenth century
were the various classes of the country so much of one mind over an
issue or a personality.

When Palmerston was dismissed from the Foreign Office in 1851,
the Queen asked the Prime Minister, Lord John Russell, for a statement of the principles upon which foreign policy would be conducted
in the future. The new Foreign Secretary, Earl Granville, duly obliged
with a 'General Statement of Policy' in January 1852.

1 (Document D) ... it is the duty and interest of this country, having possessions scattered over the whole globe, and priding itself on its
advanced state of civilisation, to encourage moral, intellectual and phys-
ical progress among all other nations. For this purpose the Foreign
5 Policy of Great Britain should be marked by justice, moderation, and self

respect, and this country should in her relations with other states do by others as it would be done by. While the Cabinet do not believe that all considerations of a higher character are to be sacrificed to the pushing of our manufactures by any means into every possible corner of the
10 globe, yet considering the great natural advantages of our Foreign Commerce, and the powerful means of civilisation it affords, one of the first duties of a British Government must always be to obtain for our Foreign Trade that security which is essential to its success ... With regard to occurrences likely to have international consequences, no
15 general rule can uniformly be applied. In each case, the Government must exercise its own discretion, whether it shall interfere at one, or remain aloof till its arbitration or good offices be required ... it will also often be found advisable to combine with other great Powers, when no sacrifice of principle is required, to settle the disputes which may arise
20 between other   nations ...

In 1849, Palmerston had already given the following general statement of principles of the conduct of policy:

1 (Document E) ... It is most desirable that foreign nations should know that, on the one hand, England is sincerely desirous to preserve and maintain peace - that we entertain no feelings of hostility towards any nation in the world - that we wish to be on the most friendly footing
5 with all - that we have a deep interest in the preservation of peace, because we are desirous to carry on with advantage those innocent and peaceful relations of commerce ... that we know must be injured by the interruption of our friendly relations with other countries; but, on the other hand, it is also essential for the protection of that commerce to
10 which we attach so much importance, that it should be known and well understood by every nation on the face of the earth that we are not disposed to submit to wrong, and the maintenance of peace on our part is subject to the indispensable condition that all countries shall respect our honour and our dignity, and shall not inflict any injury upon our
15 interests.

Reading through these documents should give an indication of the extent to which ideas on foreign policy rested on the precedents set by earlier events and individuals. Palmerston always insisted that he framed his policies in line with the principles set down by Canning - yet in his speech Peel seems to clearly suggest that Palmerston is not in line with Canningite ideas. Peel also seems to dismiss the idea that Castlereagh and Canning represented different approaches to foreign policy. Going back further than the scope of this book, Peel refers to Fox and Pitt, the bitterest of political rivals in the period 1783-1806 as following the same principles in their approach to foreign questions. Gladstone's comments indicate the emergence of a new 'moral' approach to foreign policy - note how he picks up on Palmerston's use of a classical parallel with the Roman Empire to turn the argument towards the kind of moral debate of 'do unto others as you would have them do to you' which was to become the hallmark of his thinking in future years. Bear these points in mind as you approach the questions set on these documents at the end of this chapter.

7 Palmerston Versus the Crown

The last years of Palmerston's tenure of the Foreign Office were marked by a spectacular running battle between himself and the Crown in the shape of Queen Victoria and Prince Albert. This conflict ended with Palmerston's dismissal from the Foreign Office at the end of 1851. After this he never returned to day-to-day control of foreign affairs, although as Prime Minister 1855-8 and again 1859-65 he effectively had the last word on foreign policy over the various individuals who acted as foreign secretary.

The origins of the confrontation between Palmerston and the court over the conduct of foreign policy go back to his earliest years at the Foreign Office. Constitutionally the monarch had the right to see all diplomatic despatches and to make alterations to them before they were sent. This reflected the constitutional assumption that the Crown had a particular and legitimate right and duty to oversee foreign affairs. This concept rested on the idea that all monarchs were of equal status before God and were in effect the ultimate arbiters of their respective peoples. Therefore it followed that they were the final authority on whether there was to be war or peace between their own and other nations. Obviously the emergence of constitutional states such as Britain, where the monarch shared power with other elements in the constitution such as parliaments, undermined this rather simplistic approach. However, in the British political system of the early nineteenth century the monarch still retained considerable political authority generally and it is not therefore surprising that the monarch's role in foreign affairs was still a serious issue.

From the start, Palmerston had little patience with this aspect of the work of the Foreign Office. Whilst William IV ruled from 1830 to 1837, he had little option but to accept the practice of royal supervision of despatches since William regarded it as automatic. William did change despatches on occasions and Palmerston had no real choice but to abide by the changes. However, when Victoria succeeded her uncle in 1837, Palmerston began to change the usual procedure. Instead of sending all despatches for royal approval he sent only a sample which he selected from the whole. Palmerston later justified his departure from accepted practice by arguing that the 18-year-old Queen could not be expected to deal with the onerous burden of reading all the output from the Foreign Office. It is more than probable that Palmerston was quite genuine in his desire to protect the Queen - concern about the impact of such a burden of state affairs on a very young women was fairly general in the higher political world. Also it should be remembered that Palmerston's early relations with the Queen were quite good. Before she married and came under the sobering influence of Prince Albert, the Queen was very much a social animal. She loved parties and dancing and since Palmerston, among his many talents, was an excellent dancer, she often sought him out as a partner.

However, two things happened to put Palmerston on the wrong side of the Queen. The first, predictably perhaps, was an incident with a lady-in-waiting at Windsor Castle, who subsequently complained to the Queen that Palmerston had forced his attentions upon her. The second was the Queen's marriage in 1840 to Prince Albert. The first matter might have been forgotten, but the arrival of Albert at the British court had a more profound effect. Albert was the same age as Victoria but, understandably in a male-dominated age, he had much more experience of the world and knowledge of politics. He was also intelligent and determined to be more than a decorative adornment to his new wife's entourage. He had studied the political system of his new country and had a sound knowledge of international affairs as well as many of his own private contacts at the courts of Europe. From the start of their marriage, Albert began to act as Victoria's confidential adviser and private secretary. He had a clear sense of constitutional propriety and advised her wisely in terms of her relations with the leading politicians. He played an important part in making the Queen realise that her personal dislike of Sir Robert Peel and friendship with Lord Melbourne must not spill over into political matters. However, in foreign affairs he felt that the Crown should still play an active role and he also believed that his contacts and knowledge of the foreign courts could be of use in the conduct of foreign policy.

The first problems over actual policy between the court and Palmerston arose in 1840-41 during the second Mehemet Ali crisis. Albert disliked Palmerston's policy of isolating France. He had his own contacts with the French court through King Leopold of Belgium and after the crisis was over he urged an immediate rapprochement with France to rebuild relations - Palmerston ignored this. At the same time the question of Palmerston's methods in respect of despatches came to light. Albert realised almost at once that Palmerston was not submitting all despatches to the Queen before sending them off, a point which the Queen had quite failed to grasp previously. In October 1840, Albert wrote to Palmerston informing him that the Queen required all despatches to be submitted for approval in future. Palmerston promised to see that this was done.

However, before this new relationship could be put to the test Lord Melbourne's Whig government fell and was replaced by a Conservative administration under Sir Robert Peel. This meant that Palmerston was replaced at the Foreign Office by Lord Aberdeen. The Queen and Albert found the foreign policy pursued by Peel and

Aberdeen much more to their liking. Albert was a great admirer of Peel in general and he particularly approved Aberdeen's policy of a closer relationship with Louis-Philippe. Thus when the Peel government fell in the summer of 1846 following the great crisis over the repeal of the Corn Laws, Victoria and Albert were not best pleased to see Palmerston return to the Foreign Office in Lord John Russell's Whig administration.

The next few years became virtually a running battle between the Royals and Palmerston. In 1846-7 a civil war broke out in Portugal between constitutionalists and forces loyal to Queen Maria who had tried to impose a dictatorship. Maria's husband was a German Prince who was related to both Victoria and Albert and they strongly supported her position. However, Palmerston supported the constitutionalists and used his influence to prevent intervention in Portugal, especially from the Spanish government, which regarded the Portuguese liberals as dangerous extremists. To avoid conflicts with the Queen, Palmerston began sending off some of the more sensitive Portuguese despatches without prior submission. When Victoria discovered this a sharp reprimand was sent to Palmerston who expressed his regret and blamed the Foreign Office staff for the 'oversights'. But the disagreement over Portugal was only the first of a series of clashes. The Queen began insisting on making alterations to many drafts of despatches before approving them to be sent out and Palmerston grew increasingly impatient. From time to time he still sent despatches without approval and the complaints from the Queen grew more frequent and sharper in tone.

When, early in 1848, a revolution in France deposed Louis-Philippe and set up a republic, Palmerston quickly decided to follow a policy of friendship to the new regime. This infuriated Victoria and Albert who were as hostile to the idea of a republican France as they had been friendly to the France of Louis-Philippe. In September 1848 the Queen decided formally to ask the Prime Minister, Lord John Russell, to remove Palmerston from the Foreign Office. Russell was in a dilemma. He tended to agree with Victoria and Albert that Palmerston was too independent in his actions but did not want a confrontation with him. Palmerston's increasing support for constitutional movements abroad was endearing him to the radicals in the House of Commons. The support of these radicals was an important element in the strength of Russell's government - offending Palmerston could be a fatal mistake. As a compromise Russell suggested that Palmerston might be made Leader of the House of Commons while he himself would take over the Foreign Office and go to the House of Lords. Palmerston rejected this proposal.

When the Don Pacifico controversy blew up in the summer of 1850, Victoria and Albert entertained hopes that at last their adversary would be forced to resign, especially since a motion censuring his policy was carried in the House of Lords. However, Palmerston's triumph in the Commons put him in a stronger position than ever and Russell was compelled to give him unconditional support to continue as Foreign Secretary. Russell was now hoping that the Queen would not press for his removal any more. However, Albert was determined not to let the matter die. He raised the matter of Palmerston's personal morality (or rather his lack of it), citing the attempted rape of the lady at Windsor Castle, and drafted a new demand that all despatches be submitted to the Queen. This memorandum was cast in very strong terms and Russell feared that Palmerston might resign over it, but instead the Foreign Secretary backed off and promised to abide by the correct procedure in future.

It was a temporary respite. In September 1850, the Austrian General Haynau visited Britain. He was despised for having carried out atrocities, including the flogging of women, during the Austrian repression of the 1848 revolutions in Italy and Hungary. During the visit he was set upon by workers at a brewery in London which he was being shown round and beaten up before eventually being rescued by the police. The Queen and Albert were highly sympathetic to the Austrian suppression of the 1848 revolts. The Queen described Haynau as 'one of the Emperor's distinguished Generals' and demanded that the government send an apology. Palmerston detested Haynau and was privately delighted that the brutal General had got what most public opinion in the country saw as his just deserts. However, he agreed that diplomatic protocol required that a formal apology be sent. He drafted a despatch which, whilst duly recording the government's regret for the incident, expressed the view that it had been ill-advised for Haynau to come to Britain in the first place, given the strength of public feeling against him. He also advised the Austrian government not to press for the prosecution of the brewery workers, since a trial would bring up the whole question of Haynau's atrocities in Italy and Hungary. Palmerston showed the Queen the draft version only after sending the despatch off to Vienna. The Queen's anger at this transcended anything which had gone before. She demanded that a further apology be sent in effect cancelling the first version and deleting all critical comment on Haynau. Palmerston at first seemed set to make this a resignation issue but in the end thought better of it and a new despatch was sent. However, this bizarre episode only underlined the confusion which the continuing clash was causing.

In the summer of 1851 there was more trouble. During the 1848-9 revolts a number of political refugees from Poland and Hungary, including some prominent leaders, had escaped from the Russian and Austrian army's clutches and taken refuge in Turkey. The Russians and Austrians wanted these refugees either handed over to them or at least interned permanently by the Turks. Palmerston had been using his influence with the Turks to secure the release of these refugees to travel to freedom wherever they might please. He had even promised the Turks support in the event that the Russians and Austrians took action against Turkey. The decision of the USA to offer the refugees asylum and send the US navy to collect them finally induced the Turks to agree to their release. However, Louis Kossuth, the Hungarian revolutionary leader, and a few of his close followers opted to come to Britain rather than the USA. When his ship docked at Southampton he received a tumultuous reception and was entertained to a banquet at the Guildhall. He was then brought up to London in triumph by a group of prominent radicals, stopping for several more celebratory banquets along the way.

The Queen was furious at all this fuss in support of Kossuth whom she and Albert saw as a dangerous revolutionary and was even more incensed when the *Morning Post* stated that Kossuth was to call on Palmerston to thank him for all he had done to help secure the release of the refugees. Such a meeting would have appeared to be an official governmental endorsement of the Hungarian cause, and as such a direct insult to the Austrians. The Queen demanded of Russell that Palmerston under no circumstances meet with Kossuth. Russell himself and several members of the Cabinet also thought that this would be a mistake and so Russell formally asked his Foreign Secretary to avoid the meeting. However, Palmerston at first refused Russell's request. Russell then asked the Queen to issue a direct order to Palmerston forbidding him to meet Kossuth. When this was sent to him, Palmerston for the first time seemed set to meet the court head on by replying that he would not be dictated to over whom he might invite to his own home. At the beginning of November 1851 Russell raised the matter in a Cabinet meeting and the whole Cabinet approved an instruction to Palmerston not to meet with Kossuth. Faced with this Palmerston did back down, but within a few days he had exacted revenge. Just two days after the Cabinet meeting, Palmerston received a deputation from the London boroughs of Finsbury and Islington. Both these boroughs had very radical reputations, particularly Finsbury, which had been one of the few constituencies to have returned a Chartist MP during the great years of that movement. The deputation formally thanked Palmerston for having saved the Polish and Hungarian refugees from the Emperors of Russia and Austria who were described in the address as 'despots', 'tyrants' and 'odious assassins'. Palmerston replied thanking the deputation for the honour they had done him and saying that he could not, of course, officially endorse the language used about foreign sovereigns. These proceedings were reported in the press and Victoria and Albert reflected bitterly that this was worse than if Palmerston had actually met Kossuth. However, Russell knew that to take any action against Palmerston over this issue was impossible given the popularity of Kossuth with the British public and most of the press.

The Kossuth affair strained Palmerston's relations with his Prime Minister and Cabinet colleagues and his fall from office was now imminent. At the beginning of December 1851 there was a new *coup d'état* in Paris in which Louis Napoleon seized power in effect as a dictator of France. This produced a situation where, for once, Palmerston found himself isolated from popular opinion and therefore vulnerable. The radicals and most of the Liberals were fiercely opposed to the coup as were some Conservatives. Palmerston found himself in support of a Bonapartist dictatorship along with the more arch-Tory politicians who felt that Louis Napoleon was the only hope of avoiding the triumph of socialism in France. Even Wellington, who had once done perhaps as much as any single figure to destroy Bonapartism now wrote, 'France needs a Napoleon'. Palmerston believed that Louis Napoleon was the best option in a situation in which the alternatives were socialism, anarchy or the restoration of Louis-Philippe - none of which appealed to him.

In such confused circumstances it was perhaps rash of Palmerston to respond to the coup with a clear private expression of support for Louis Napoleon. He also communicated his view in a private letter to the British Ambassador in Paris. When, therefore, the Cabinet decided on a policy of strict neutrality in relation to the events in France, Palmerston was left exposed. Although he tried to retrieve the situation by sending a formal despatch setting out the government's position, the new French regime claimed that it had already been recognised by Palmerston, and the British Ambassador, who actually did not like Palmerston very much, confirmed that this was his understanding of the situation. Victoria and Albert were quick to spot Palmerston's vulnerability. It only required the revelation that Palmerston had yet again sent another (fairly minor) despatch to Paris without prior submission to the Queen for them to demand his resignation. This time Russell and the Cabinet were in agreement that Palmerston was acting too independently and Russell insisted that he leave the Foreign Office and go to Ireland as Lord-Lieutenant with a full UK peerage. Palmerston refused point-blank to do this and on 26 December 1851 he ceased to be Foreign Secretary. Within a few weeks he had struck back in what he famously described as a 'tit-for-tat with John Russell'. In a debate on defence in February 1852, he moved an amendment in the House of Commons to a Government Bill to provide for local militia to be set up in the counties. Palmerston argued for a national militia and his amendment was carried against the government resulting in Russell's resignation.

This whole saga demonstrates the peculiar way in which Britain's relations with the European powers became entangled in this period with the changing constitutional reality of relations between the Crown and the government of the day. Victoria, encouraged by Albert, was attempting to maintain the idea that foreign policy should be seen in a different light to the political issues involved in domestic affairs. In the domestic sphere it was clear that royal influence was going to be strictly limited to an advisory role. Albert, however, believed that international affairs were no matter for popular influence and public approval or politicians' and parties' policies. He hoped to carve out a specific place for an active Crown involvement in this area and he impressed on Victoria this vision. It was something of an illusion even at the time and in the longer term there was never any prospect that this one sphere of political life could somehow be detached from the rest of the political agenda and preserved as a royal prerogative. Palmerston's fall in 1851 came about primarily not because of the Queen's disapproval of his actions but because he had alienated his cabinet colleagues and isolated himself from the support which had sustained him through his previous clashes with the Crown. Most significantly, the whole episode, along with the Don Pacifico controversy, shows us the increasing importance of public opinion in the formation of the government's foreign policy. While Palmerston was in tune with popular sentiments he was secure - when he struck a discordant note he lost the office he had dominated for the majority of the past two decades.

Making notes on 'Palmerston and the Changing Scene in Europe'

The key theme in this chapter has been to show the period as a transitional one in which British policy was adjusting to new circumstances.
You should consider the following points:
1. How did relations with a) France, and b) Russia, change during this period and what factors caused these changes?
2. How did Palmerston deal with the problems he faced over:
a) Belgium,
b) Turkey (use Chapter 5 as well),
c) The 1848 Revolutions and their aftermath, and
d) Crown interference in foreign policy?
3. Did Palmerston adopt any consistent principles in his handling of foreign policy?
4. What role did the press and public play in determining the course of foreign policy in this period?

Answering essay questions on 'Palmerston and the Changing Scene in Europe'

Example: 'An opportunist and a bully rather than a great statesman.' Is this a fair assessment of Palmerston's policy in European affairs 1830-51?
Almost all the questions posed on Palmerston in this period are variations on this theme. The question invites you to discuss whether Palmerston was a Foreign Secretary who only acted firmly when dealing with weaker powers, i.e. the characteristic of a 'bully' being to attack those who cannot fight back, whilst deferring to those likely to inflict some retaliation. 'Opportunism' is a concept often chosen as

the basis of 'A' level essay questions in a wide variety of contexts and is taken to mean that actions or policies are decided upon not because of their intrinsic merits but because they fit the needs of the moment or the interests of the individual concerned. Defining a 'statesman' often seems to cause difficulty for students. A basic definition would be: one who has skill and experience in the conduct of public affairs. However, the term has come to mean also that the individual so described has qualities of rising above personal or party interests and takes decisions on higher issues of humanity, putting aside petty issues and interests. Most quotes used in exams are usually made up by the Chief Examiner - or cribbed from other Chief Examiners! - so do not be afraid to be critical of the quote if you see the opportunity. In Palmerston's case one famous quote from Disraeli has, in fact, often been taken out of context. 'Ginger Beer rather than Champagne' is a lovely description typical of Disraeli which he once used of Palmerston. However, the quote, generally used as a verdict on Palmerston's foreign policy, was actually intended by Disraeli as a verdict on Palmerston's performance in one particular debate - Disraeli was basically an admirer of Palmerston, though party allegiance meant that he was not inclined to show this too obviously. Once again the above example shows the importance of precision in defining terms used in questions.

Source-based questions on 'Palmerston and the Changing Scene in Europe'

Refer to the documents on pages 74-7 and answer the following questions.

a) In Document A, to what is Palmerston referring when he speaks of a 'political earthquake rolling Europe from side to side'? (5 marks)

b) By what arguments is Palmerston attempting to convince his listeners to support his handling of foreign policy in Document A? (5 marks)

c) Sum up in your own words the nature of Gladstone's opposition to Palmerston as shown in Document B. (5 marks)

d) Comparing Document B with Document C, in what ways does Peel's attitude to Palmerston's foreign policy differ from that of Gladstone? (10 marks)

e) To what extent can you detect in Document D any influence of the ideas expressed in the first three documents? (10 marks)

f) Comparing Document D with Document E, would you conclude that any fundamental change in the principles of British foreign policy is indicated by Earl Granville's statement? (5 marks)

g) To what extent do these documents, taken together, justify the view that there were fundamental differences in approach to foreign policy issues amongst politicians? (15 marks)

Summary Diagram

Palmerston and the Changing Scene in Europe, 1830-51

Domestic Affairs
Reform crisis: Passing of the Great Reform Act 1831-2
1833-48: Social reform. Factories, health, education, poor relief, police, local government are targets
1838-48: Chartism
1846: Campaign for the repeal of the Corn Laws
1830-41: Political dominance of the Whigs
1830-46: the rise of Peel's Conservative Party and its fall in 1846

1830: Palmerston became Foreign Secretary
1831-3: Crisis in Low Countries and Turkey Britain intervened in the former but not the latter

1833: Treaty of Unkiar Skelessi - reversed by Palmerston in Second Mehemet Ali Crisis
1839-41: Palmerston confirmed support for constitutionalism against the principles of the Holy Alliance in the Quadruple Alliance with France, Spain and Portugal 1834

1841-6: Aberdeen sought closer relationships with France
1846: Tsar visited London and misinterpreted British attitude to the Eastern Question

1846: Palmerston returned as Foreign Secretary
1848: Revolutions in Europe
1846-51: Clash between Palmerston and the Crown over the conduct of foreign policy ended in his resignation as Foreign Secretary

5 Britain and the Eastern Question, 1815-65

1 The Nature of the Eastern Question

By 1815 the status of the Turkish Empire (otherwise known as the Ottoman Empire) as a 'sick man' was well-established. The essence of the problem, from the viewpoint of the great powers of Europe, was that an Islamic and Asiatic power was imposing a corrupt, inefficient and frequently brutal rule upon millions of Christians in a large area of south-eastern Europe. The European powers had never accepted the Turks as being of equal status to themselves. But, despite the collective assumption of racial superiority, as the Turkish Empire weakened during the eighteenth century, no commonly acceptable policy could be found which would allow a consensus to emerge on how to deal with the problem. On the one hand, the wish to see fellow Christians liberated from Islamic rule inclined the great powers to welcome the signs of decline; on the other, there was a fear that conflicting interests amongst the powers themselves would lead to war if Turkey collapsed without there being any agreement on how to fill the 'power vacuum' which would be created on its demise. Thus, although the general attitude of the European powers towards Turkey was one of disdain for its notorious corruption and inefficiency and its presumed barbarism, they had to face the fact that the maintenance of Turkish integrity might be preferable to a war between the powers themselves over the disposal of Turkish possessions. As Turkey continued to decline, so the European powers were faced with an ongoing problem in relation to the balance of power and stability of international relations - how would the former territories of the Turkish Empire be divided up in the event of a collapse?

In the eighteenth century Britain had attached relatively little importance to the question of the future of Turkey. Britain had enjoyed a healthy trading relationship with Turkey since the sixteenth century, but this was not of sufficient size to be considered of great significance. When Russia defeated Turkey in a war in 1774 and imposed a punitive peace settlement under the Treaty of Kutchuk-Kainardji on the Turks, the event aroused little interest in Britain. In contrast there was immediate consternation in France, where the need to protect a valuable source of foreign trade with Turkey caused the French to protest vehemently to the Russians. However, the increasing importance of the Indian Empire towards the end of the century gradually began to change this relative British indifference, and the loss of the American colonies in the 1780s prompted a general reconsideration of the security of other British imperial possessions. The event which changed British perceptions most dramatically, however, was the invasion of the Turkish dependency of Egypt by Napoleon Bonaparte at the end of the 1790s. This threatened British links with the East and forced a response. Bonaparte was eventually expelled from Egypt by British military and naval power, but the lesson was not forgotten and the future of Turkey accordingly became an issue for British interests at the Vienna Congress.

By the time the Vienna Congress met in late 1814, the situation surrounding British attitudes towards Turkey was complex. Castlereagh was concerned to safeguard the ailing Empire, but he also wanted to fit Turkey into the wider needs of the balance of power in Europe. The overwhelming priority for Britain was to prevent the resurgence of an expansionist France and the key to this lay in the power of Russia. However, Castlereagh was also anxious that Russia should not become too strong. To guard against this the strategic positions of the countries bordering Russia were crucial. Turkey, with its hold on south-eastern Europe and on the narrow stretches of water between the Black and Mediterranean Seas (the Straits of the Bosphorus and the Dardanelles), was potentially a significant element in this complicated calculation. To make matters even more confused Britain had to recognise that the French might again, at some point in the future, become a direct threat to British interests. The future of Turkey had become an issue which bore upon British interests in a number of different ways: the security of the Indian Empire and commercial interests both there and elsewhere in the Far East; the balance of power in Europe and the maintenance of European peace and stability.

2 The Greek Wars of Independence, 1821-30

Perhaps the greatest potential threat to the future viability of the Turkish Empire, and one which lay largely outside the control of the great powers, was the danger of internal revolts against Turkish rule by subject peoples. The Greeks had long been simmering in resentment at Turkish control and, in 1821, they rose in revolt. The rising commenced with a brutal massacre of Muslims, including the execution of 12,000 Turkish troops who had already surrendered to the Greeks at Tripolitsa. Turkish retaliation followed. Greek religious leaders (who had actually condemned the revolt!) were hanged in Constantinople and most of the occupants of the Greek island of Chios were massacred. The Greeks declared themselves to be independent in January 1822.

The reaction in Britain to the Greek revolt was mixed. Naturally popular sentiment was largely with the Greeks as Christian victims of 'Muslim barbarity'. However, at the higher levels of politics, opinions were more varied. Castlereagh, recognising the extent to which the Greeks looked to the Russians as fellow Orthodox Christians for support, saw a potential clash between Russia and Turkey and urged the former to act with restraint. At the same time, he warned the Turks that Britain would not support them if they provoked a war with

Russia. However, the feelings of the Russians were running high following the executions in Constantinople and by mid-1821 Russia and Turkey were close to war. The neutralist approach which Castlereagh had adopted looked unlikely to be enough to prevent hostilities from breaking out and it was in this climate that Castlereagh and Metternich, the Austrian Chancellor, met (for what proved to be the last time) in Hanover in October 1821. To their mutual regret they found that little agreement was possible on the Greek issue. Austria was broadly sympathetic to Russia whereas Britain was not, and, in any case, both countries realised that if they appeared to be cooperating too closely it might have the opposite effect to that which was intended, and provoke the Russians rather than restraining them. The failure to find a common strategy with the Austrians on the Greek Question, though disappointing, did not appear to Castlereagh to be too alarming - he took comfort from the fact that relations between himself and Metternich, strained since their disagreement over the Troppau Protocol (see page 43), had been restored.

What benefits might have accrued from a renewed collaboration between Castereagh and Metternich must remain hypothetical. Castlereagh's suicide in August 1822 meant the end of British diplomacy based on such personal relationships. To Metternich the advent of Canning as Foreign Secretary was a disaster and the signal for him to retreat to the security of closer ties with the Russians. For his part, Canning had no desire to seek an allied approach to the Eastern Question at that time. His personal sympathies were with the Greeks, and in 1823 he accorded them formal recognition as 'belligerents' rather than 'rebels'. However, his main concern was always the best interests of Britain and, in any case, he had to contend with the influence of Wellington, who was suspicious of revolts of any kind. The King too was less than enthusiastic about Greek claims. When Alexander I tried to promote joint intervention, Canning refused to agree. However, when the Tsar died at the end of 1825 Canning saw the opportunity for a closer relationship with Russia. The new Tsar, Nicholas I, proved rather less enthusiastic for congress-style diplomacy and far more willing to engage in direct negotiations. This suited Canning and he persuaded Wellington to go to Russia with the object of securing a bilateral agreement on Greece.

The result of this initiative was the Protocol of St Petersburg of April 1826. By the terms of the Protocol, Britain and Russia agreed that Greece would become an autonomous state, but remain under Turkish suzerainty (i.e., a self-governing dependency). This agreement was followed by the Treaty of London in July 1827 and the French were also brought into the discussions. These three powers now agreed to an alliance which would force the Turks to accept Greek autonomy or, if they remained obdurate, would aim instead to secure full Greek independence.

Canning died in August 1827, but the policy which he had set in motion followed its own momentum under his feeble successor, Lord Goderich. The Turks refused an armistice and decided to quell the revolt. To do this the Sultan was forced to rely on the power of his Egyptian vassal, Mehemet Ali, an able and ruthless ruler who was more than a match for the Greeks. However, Mehemet Ali's forces in Greece had to be supplied and reinforced from Egypt and the allied navies were sent to sever this supply line. The result was the Battle of Navarino in which the Turkish and Egyptian fleets were destroyed in October 1827.

At this point a major complication set in on the British side. In January 1828, the Duke of Wellington replaced Lord Goderich as Prime Minister. He appointed Lord Aberdeen as Foreign Secretary. Aberdeen, a classical scholar of some repute, was personally sympathetic to the Greeks but Wellington, alarmed by the growing weakness of Turkey, decided on a dramatic change of policy. He formally apologised to the Sultan for the sinking of his fleet and distanced Britain from the dispute. The Sultan meanwhile repudiated a previous agreement which he had made with the Russians and declared a holy war. This act of lunacy had the inevitable effect of causing the Russians to declare war on Turkey in April 1828. The war was a complete disaster for the Turks and the Russians were able to impose a peace settlement, the Treaty of Adrianople, in September 1829. Under the terms of the settlement Turkey had to agree to what amounted to a Russian protectorate over Moldavia and Wallachia, which were situated in a vital position at the mouth of the River Danube (see the map on page 97). This meant that Turkey had given up control of an important strategic position. Additionally the Turks had to submit to various other conditions, such as Serbian autonomy under Russian protection and commercial concessions.

To Britain these arrangements seemed to portend the break-up of Turkey on Russian terms. The Treaty of Adrianople said nothing on the subject of Greece, but Wellington and Aberdeen now felt that the Greek Question could not simply be left unresolved. To Wellington this seemed to offer further opportunities for Russian pressure in the future. In reality the fears of Wellington and Aberdeen were almost entirely groundless. The Russians had themselves concluded in 1829 that the preservation of Turkey would serve their interests better than the setting up of a series of possibly unpredictable independent Balkan states. The Russians had assumed that this was what they were ensuring by the Treaty of Adrianople, which from their point of view had seemed moderate. This, however, was not perceived at the time, and Britain was joined by France and Austria in drawing the wrong conclusions from the settlement imposed by the Russians.

Wellington's solution to this dilemma was to perform another complete about-face on the Greek Question and to opt for outright Greek independence. In this he was supported by the Austrians who also distrusted Russian intentions. Metternich had objected to the more limited plans for Greek autonomy, initiated by Canning in 1826; now he joined with Britain in supporting a more drastic solution. The three allied powers, Britain, France and Russia, met in London in February 1830 to discuss the Greek Question and no difficulty was encountered in agreeing to the basic principle of independence. The three powers themselves guaranteed the borders of the new nation, under arrangements which left northern Greece and the island of Crete - previously a major centre of revolt - still in Turkish hands. It was these proposals, which meant a smaller Greek state than the Greeks were demanding, which stirred Palmerston, who was much more pro-Greek than Canning had been, into a strong condemnation of Wellington's policy and helped seal his alliance with the Whigs.

3 Palmerston and the Threats to Turkey, 1830-41

The settlement of the Greek crisis did not bring about any respite for the Turkish Empire. On the contrary, the use which the Sultan made of Mehemet Ali to subdue the Greeks ushered in the next phase of the Eastern Question and led to new difficulties for British policy. Mehemet Ali had received Crete as a reward for his services, but he was far from satisfied with this. He was anxious to secure Syria and the city of Damascus. In 1831 he sent his son Ibrahim to attack Palestine. Ibrahim had been his father's general in Greece and was a seasoned and effective campaigner. He made short work of the Sultan's forces. By the end of 1832 he had defeated the last army that Turkey could field against him and looked set to seize Constantinople and with it, in effect, the whole Turkish Empire. The Sultan, no doubt recalling Wellington's conciliatory attitude in 1828, now swallowed his pride and appealed to Britain for help.

Since the end of 1830, Palmerston had been Foreign Secretary in the Whig dominated coalition government headed by Lord Grey, and he now had to respond to this appeal. Despite his position on the issue of Greece, Palmerston was not generally anti-Turkish as such. In any case, Palmerston's reaction to specific events was governed almost entirely by his perception of how they affected British interests. In this instance his instinct was to help Turkey. He did not want to see Mehemet Ali make further gains at the expense of Turkey, since he feared (correctly) that the influence of the French lay behind the rising power of the Egyptians. In the event, however, Palmerston's ideas did not convince the Cabinet, which refused to agree to his pleas for intervention on behalf of the Sultan. The reasons for this refusal by the Cabinet were complex. Some Whigs were naturally Francophile and did not share Palmerston's suspicions of France; some saw Mehemet Ali as a reformer and therefore preferable to the Sultan; some were worried about over-extending British resources at a time when the navy was already involved in the blockade against Holland (see page 65). Palmerston was therefore compelled to inform the Sultan that no aid could be expected from Britain. He was under no illusions as to the serious implications of this decision. In later years he wrote,

1   There is nothing that has happened since I have been in this office which I regret so much as that tremendous blunder ... Grey, who was with me on the point, was weak and gave way, and so nothing was done in a crisis of the utmost importance to all Europe. (1838)
5   I humbly venture to think ... that no British Cabinet at any period of the history of England ever made so great a mistake in regard to foreign affairs. (1840)

The Sultan was left with no alternative but to swallow even greater quantities of pride and appeal to the Russians. In the words of one of his own officials it was much as 'a drowning man clings to a serpent'. Palmerston hit the same note with his own comment, 'the Russian Ambassador becomes chief Cabinet minister of the Sultan'. The help of Russia was decisive but it came at a price. A Russian squadron entering the Bosphorus in February 1833 was enough to convince Ibrahim to retreat. He was too good a general to risk a clash with the Russians. In April, 6000 Russian troops landed opposite Constantinople and the security of the Sultan was assured. This still left Ibrahim in a strong position so long as he made no further moves forward. The Russians forced the Sultan to sign a new agreement, the Treaty of Unkiar Skelessi, in July 1833, before withdrawing their troops. Under this treaty the two countries agreed to mutual assistance in the event of an attack on either one of them and the Turks agreed to close the Dardanelles to all warships whenever the Russians asked them to. The latter arrangement was, naturally enough, intended to be a secret provision, but Lord Ponsonby, the British Ambassador at Constantinople, found out about it almost immediately and notified Palmerston.

With Mehemet Ali checked, but still in a strong situation, the French urged the Sultan to make concessions to their protégé. Palmerston, trying to make the best of a bad job and preserve some semblance of British prestige, added his voice to this advice, judging that, however objectionable Mehemet Ali was, another conflict of any kind must be avoided for the time being. In public he defended the intervention of the Russians whilst behind the scenes he ordered Ponsonby to persuade the Sultan not to ratify the Treaty of Unkiar Skelessi. When this failed he sent strong protest notes to Turkey and to Russia but he still did not criticise the Russians publicly and even defended them in the House of Commons. However, Palmerston was privately outraged and worried by what had occurred. The Russians had achieved an unprecedented degree of influence over Turkey, while Mehemet Ali, with his French connections, had gained

Palestine, Syria, Aleppo and Damascus as concessions from the Sultan. What incensed Palmerston most of all was that now the Turks were pledged not to make any foreign policy decisions without consulting Russia. His frustration was made all the more difficult to bear by his belief that it was the stupidity of his own Cabinet colleagues which had brought this disaster about.

In the immediate situation following the signing of the Treaty of Unkiar Skelessi, there was little that Palmerston could do to remedy the situation. He did his best to restore good relations with the Sultan and in 1838 agreed to help Turkey resist any attempt by Mehemet Ali to declare himself independent from the Empire. This undertaking was in fact considerably less that the Sultan hoped for, since he was harbouring the idea of a pre-emptive strike against Mehemet Ali and had wanted an offensive agreement with Britain to support this. Even so the arrangement went at least some way to breaching the Turkish dependence on Russia. Finally, in April 1839, the Sultan, now aware that he was dying and determined to have revenge upon Mehemet Ali before his demise, launched an attack on Syria. It was a complete failure and the Sultan died in July. At that the Turkish fleet promptly sailed to Alexandria and surrendered to Mehemet Ali. Palmerston had done nothing to incite the Sultan to this attack and had even instructed Ponsonby to make it clear to him that he could not expect British support if he did make a move. Nevertheless, once the Sultan had disturbed the status quo, it created a situation of both danger and opportunity for Palmerston. There was the danger that the conflict might escalate into a European war; there was the opportunity for him to undo the Treaty of Unkiar Skelessi.

Palmerston now embarked on a lengthy process of diplomacy in which he showed considerable skill as well as enjoying a fair degree of luck. He accepted a call from the French to send their respective fleets jointly to the Dardanelles in order to impress the Russians who might be expected to intervene because things had gone badly for the Turks. At the same time he proposed an international conference of the five great powers. He then secured a separate Anglo-Russian agreement under which the Russians agreed to modifications in the Treaty of Unkiar Skelessi and Britain agreed to support the expulsion of Mehemet Ali from Syria. In this way Palmerston isolated the French and curbed the power of Mehemet Ali (whom he thoroughly detested) whilst over turning the provisions of Unkiar Skelessi.

It was not all plain sailing. France threatened war and the pro-French elements in Britain (including those within the Cabinet) gave Palmerston a hard time. However, he held firm to his conviction that the French would not fight to keep Mehemet Ali in Syria. He had a major stroke of good fortune when the Syrians themselves revolted against Ibrahim and loosened his hold upon the region. The result was two conventions which secured virtually all that Palmerston could have hoped for. The London Convention - which the French refused to sign - expelled Mehemet Ali from Syria, and he was subsequently compelled under threat from the Royal Navy to return the Turkish fleet. To compensate him for the loss of Syria, Mehemet Ali was raised to the status of hereditary ruler of Egypt. The Straits Convention was signed in 1841. Under this, the major powers and Turkey agreed that the Straits (i.e. the Bosphorus and the Dardanelles) would be closed to all warships while Turkey was at peace. These arrangements established a situation which was very much in British interests. The French had been diplomatically out-manoeuvred and their protégé Mehemet Ali had been removed as a future threat. By the 1850s Egypt was one of the weakest provinces of the Turkish Empire. Moreover, Britain was once again regarded as the principal diplomatic ally of Turkey and Russian influence had declined.

4 The Crimean War, 1854-6

The next great crisis of the Eastern Question was created not by anything which occurred within the Turkish Empire, but by a deterioration in relationships between the great powers themselves. There were a number of factors involved and the issues largely lay outside British control. The Holy Alliance powers, Austria, Prussia and Russia, drifted apart due to the dislocating effects of the revolutions in Europe during 1848-9. The Austrians resented having to rely on Russian support to crush their own rebels in Hungary. At the same time the Austrians were increasingly worried about future Prussian intentions in the German states. In addition, the Russians regarded the French Emperor, Napoleon III, who had created the Second French Empire by *coup d'état* in 1851, as a 'non-legitimate' sovereign. Napoleon, sensitive to any suggestion that he was not a bona fide monarch, duly reciprocated the Tsar's dislike. At the same time Anglo-Russian relations, which had become excellent during the 1840s, began to founder in mistrust. Thus when Napoleon III, seeking to increase his popularity at home, chose to raise the issue of French rights of protection over the Roman Catholic monks in the Holy Places in Palestine - which was part of the Turkish Empire - all the ingredients for war were present.

Of all the developments which contributed to the outbreak of the Crimean War in 1854, the breakdown of Anglo-Russian relations was perhaps the most serious. In both 1826 and 1839 it had been the willingness of first Canning and then Palmerston to secure the cooperation of Russia, and the willingness of the Russians to respond, which had opened the door to settlement. Although Palmerston retained a watchful eye on any sign of expansion of Russian influence, he was never fundamentally anti-Russian. The signing of the Straits Convention meant, so far as Britain was concerned, the restoration of the old status quo and the prospect of sound long-term understanding with Russia. This was certainly the view which Lord

Aberdeen took when he returned to the Foreign Office in 1841 following the fall of the Whig government in the General Election. When the Tsar visited London in 1844, it coincided with a period of extremely bad relations between Britain and France, which were giving rise to genuine fears that there might be war between them. Peel and Aberdeen took the opportunity to seek a closer understanding with the Russians. This took the form of an agreement that both powers would seek, as their first aim of policy, to preserve the integrity of Turkey, but if that should prove impossible they would consult each other on how to proceed. In the longer term it might have been better if these talks had never taken place. To the Tsar, they seemed to guarantee that he had an understanding with Aberdeen, who became Prime Minister at the end of 1852. However, in Britain, the publication of the details in 1854 led to claims that Russia had intrigued over a long period to bring about the dismemberment of Turkey.

A number of factors caused the breakdown in Anglo-Russian relations. The brutal actions of Russia in assisting Austria to put down a revolt in Hungary in 1849 angered public opinion, which was always inclined to be anti-Russian anyway. The British blockade of Greece during the Don Pacifico affair (see page 74), which was carried out without giving notice to the other great powers, offended the Russians. Turkey, anxious now to retain the security of British protection, regularly expressed concern about future Russian aggression. Finally, the Tsar himself, apparently feeling that he had a complete understanding with the British, frequently expressed ideas concerning the hypothetical occupations of Egypt (by Britain) and Constantinople (by Russia), which sowed confusion and doubt about his aims.

It was, however, the intervention of France over the Holy Places which stirred the Tsar into action. In March 1853 he sent Prince Menshikov to Constantinople. His mission was to force the Sultan to repudiate the concessions to France and to gain further rights for Russia as protector of all the Orthodox Christians within the Turkish Empire. In addition a Russo-Turkish defensive alliance was demanded. The Sultan agreed to withdraw his concessions to France, but was persuaded by the British Ambassador, Sir Stratford Canning, to reject all the other demands. This naturally angered Menshikov and he departed from Constantinople in protest, as he had previously threatened to do if Russian requirements were not met in full. In July Russia occupied Moldavia and Wallachia whilst at the same time the Tsar stated that he wished not for war but merely to secure recognition of Russian religious rights. The occupation of Moldavia and Wallachia, which bordered the Austrian Empire, alienated the Austrians who mobilised troops in response. Turkey, however, acting on British advice, did not resist. Britain, France and Austria now joined in constructing a peace formula which became known as the Vienna Note. The three powers hoped by this to pacify the Russians by reaffirming Russia's right to sail her ships in the Black Sea and through the Straits into the Mediterranean, and by obtaining further guarantees from the Turks that decisions relating to the Turkish rule over Christian subjects would not be made without reference first to either France or Russia. At first the Tsar appeared satisfied, but an attempt by the Sultan to modify the terms so as to make them less humiliating undermined this agreement and by October 1853 the situation had become deadlocked.

As the crisis drifted on, the Turks stiffened their resolve and took the initiative. At the beginning of October 1853, the Sultan demanded that Russia withdraw its forces from Moldavia and Wallachia. When the Russians predictably refused to comply, Turkey declared war. At first Britain, along with France, made an attempt at neutrality, but when the Turkish fleet was totally destroyed at Sinope (see the map on page 97) at the end of November 1853, the pressure for British intervention grew. Public opinion was already violently anti-Russian and the Sinope victory was presented in the press as 'barbarism' following allegations (probably false) that the Russians had massacred the Turks after they had already surrendered. The British and French fleets entered the Black Sea in January 1854. The Russians asked for clarification of Anglo-French intentions and, receiving no satisfactory reply, withdrew their ambassadors from London and Paris. At the end of February Britain and France demanded the withdrawal of Russian troops from Moldavia and Wallachia and, receiving no response, made a treaty of alliance with Turkey on 12 March 1854. On 18 March war was declared by Britain and France on Russia.

In the House of Commons on 31 March 1854 Lord John Russell announced the declaration of war and justified it in the following terms:

1 For the period of more than forty years this country has been in the enjoyment of the blessings of peace, and those blessings have never been more widely nor more extensively valued. The privileges of the people have been increased, their burdens have been diminished, and,
5 with an increasing and prosperous commerce wealth has been diffused throughout the country ... I shall endeavour ... to point to the course which Russia has pursued, and to show that, unless we are content to submit to the future aggrandisement of that Power, and, possibly, to the destruction of Turkey - whose integrity and independence have been so
10 often declared essential to the stability of the system of Europe - we have no choice left us but to interpose by arms ... There are, I know, some who think that this country might remain altogether apart from the conflicts of other European nations; ... But we ... are following the maxim which ... has governed and actuated the councils of this country
15 - we who have believed that we have a part to play in the great question of the liberties and independence of Europe ... we who have seen

The Eastern Question, 1815-56

this country rise to power, rise to reputation, rise I may also say to moral greatness ... we are not prepared to abandon our position in Europe ...

John Bright, a Radical MP and veteran campaigner for Free Trade and international harmony, sounded a dissenting voice:

1 If the phrase of the 'balance of power' is to be used as an argument for war peace can never be secure. ... The past events of our history have taught us that the intervention of this country in European wars is not only unnecessary, but calamitous; that we have rarely come out of such
5 intervention having succeeded in the objects we fought for: that a debt of £800,000,000 sterling has been incurred by the policy which the noble Lord approves ... and ... we have left Europe at least as much in chains as before a single effort was made by us to rescue her from tyranny ... I believe if this country ... had adopted the principle of non-
10 intervention in every case where her interests were not directly and obviously assailed ... This country might have been a garden, every dwelling might have been of marble ... We might have had neither Trafalgar nor Waterloo but we should have set a high example of a Christian nation, free in its isolation ... and resting its policy on the
15 unchangeable foundations of Christian morality.

None of the great powers had really anticipated that a major war would result from a dispute over the Holy Places. With the possible exception of France, none of the powers saw any likely benefits which might be gained. The war resulted from the general confusion and indecision which beset European diplomacy in the early 1850s. Nowhere was this more obvious than in Britain; indeed the British position was decisive only in as much as it confused both the Russians and the Turks, making conflict more likely. In the former case, the Tsar was misled into thinking that Britain was not prepared to fight; in the latter case, the Sultan was misled into thinking that British intervention was almost a formality. That such misconceptions could arise was due to the lack of firm control over foreign policy, which in turn resulted from the confused domestic political situation.

   This destabilisation of British foreign policy began at the end of 1851 when Palmerston was forced to resign from the Foreign Office. As explained in the previous chapter his fall was prompted by his incautious private approval of Louis Napoleon's coup given to the French Ambassador in London (see page 83). This was at odds with the official government policy which had decided upon a neutral response to the seizure of power and gave Queen Victoria grounds to secure her long-desired removal of Palmerston from the Foreign Office. The Cabinet scarcely had time to adjust to life without Palmerston before it too fell, brought down by Palmerston's condemnation in the House of Commons of an ineffectual defence policy. For most of 1852 foreign policy was in the hands of Lord Malmesbury who took office in a minority Conservative administration headed by Lord Derby. Palmerston knew Malmesbury well and had strong connections with his family, so he frequently advised the new Foreign Secretary from behind the scenes. However, the new government did not last. At the end of 1852 Lord Aberdeen became Prime Minister, forming a Whig-Peelite coalition, in which Palmerston, still unacceptable so far as the Foreign Office was concerned, agreed to become Home Secretary.

The new government had a wealth of talent and experience at its disposal, but in terms of foreign policy it contained a fatal excess of riches. In his biography of Palmerston, Jasper Ridley, observed that to have Palmerston in the Cabinet, but not at the Foreign Office, was an arrangement likely to produce the worst possible results. Palmerston was certain to try to impose his influence in the conduct of foreign affairs. However, he faced powerful rivals within the Cabinet. Lord John Russell, who went to the Foreign Office initially, was a former Prime Minister; his successor as Foreign Secretary, Lord Clarendon, was a former diplomat, profoundly anti-Turkish and dominated by the greater figures around him, especially Palmerston and Aberdeen. The Prime Minister himself, of course, was a former Foreign Secretary, with a quite different approach to foreign policy from that of Palmerston. If this were not enough, the Chancellor of the Exchequer was William Ewart Gladstone, now a formidable political figure in his own right, and deeply opposed to what he saw as the immorality of Palmerston's attitude to foreign policy.

In these circumstances it can scarcely be considered surprising that British policy went through a confused and ineffectual period. Within the Cabinet, Palmerston attempted to force through a tough but unequivocal approach of resisting Russian expansion and supporting Turkey. However, since he was not at the Foreign Office itself, he was unable to achieve any consistency in direction and control. Clarendon, who took over the Foreign Office in February 1853, showed himself to be suspicious of the Turks, arguing that they were seeking to entangle Britain in their problems, which to his mind were in no small measure due to their consistent failure to initiate reforms which Britain had consistently urged on them. However, Clarendon found it impossible to control the independent policy adopted by the British Ambassador at Constantinople, Sir Stratford Canning. The cousin of the late, great Foreign Secretary and Prime Minister had long been accustomed to making on-the-spot decisions and, although he had dutifully followed official policy in pressing the Sultan to introduce reforms, he went well beyond his authority in constantly urging the Turks to adopt an intransigent resistance to the Russians and in assuring them of the certainty of British support. Both Aberdeen and Clarendon seriously considered removing Canning from his post but took no action. This, in turn, confirmed in the Sultan's mind the idea that Canning's assurances carried the

WHAT IT HAS COME TO.

Aberdeen. "I MUST LET HIM GO!"

Punch shows Lord Aberdeen as having attempted to restrain the aggressive Lion of England. Aberdeen is saying 'I must let him go.'

force of the British government's concurrence.

When news of the destruction of the Turkish fleet at Sinope broke in Britain in mid-December 1853, it was followed almost immediately by the resignation of Palmerston. In reality the two events were unrelated - Palmerston had resigned over a disagreement with Russell who was advocating that the government bring in a new measure of parliamentary reform. However, the public assumption was that Palmerston had gone in protest against the government's failure to react more strongly to the alleged Russian atrocities. Palmerston did nothing to correct this view because he quickly saw that the misinterpretation of his actions brought more pressure on the government to adopt a tougher line. The Tsar was also misled. Although Aberdeen did send a stiff note of protest about Sinope, Palmerston's departure reassured him that the response was a matter of form, and that what he had come to regard as his 'understanding' with Britain remained valid.

Palmerston's resignation was a brief affair. After ten days he resumed his post at the Home Office, creating even more confusion over whether this represented a concession on his part or on Aberdeen's. His return was at the instigation of the Prime Minister, who wrote to him specifically urging him to withdraw his resignation. Once back in the Cabinet Palmerston became even more convinced that Aberdeen was dangerously pacific in his dealings with the Russians and that they would only understand a firm approach. His fears led him to take a more aggressive attitude in Cabinet than he would probably have done had control of policy been in his own hands.

The Crimean War quickly degenerated into a costly and embarrassing stalemate. Although there were victories over the Russians at Balaclava and Inkerman to celebrate, these were essentially defensive triumphs in which attacks by superior numbers of Russian troops were repulsed only with heavy casualties. To set against this there was mounting public anger over the reports of heavy losses resulting from the poor sanitary and medical conditions suffered by British soldiers. By the end of January 1855, the pressure on the government was becoming unbearable. Aberdeen was tired and sickened by the whole business and when Parliament reassembled after the Christmas recess his government faced a demand in the House of Commons that there should be a Parliamentary Committee set up to investigate the conduct of the war. This was in effect a censure motion. When the motion was carried by 305 votes to 157 the government had no option but to resign.

Palmerston was the obvious choice to lead a new government. In the country at large he was regarded as the only man capable of saving the situation, and opinion in the House of Commons was also in his favour. The Queen did not want him as Prime Minister and did her best to prevent his succession, sending first for Lord Lansdowne, then Lord Clarendon and finally Russell, before bowing to the inevitable and inviting Palmerston to form an administration. The popular view that Palmerston was the man of the hour and could alone rescue the situation was a status he scarcely merited. However, in such situations the truth is of less importance than what people believe to be the truth. The Duke of Argyll, a member of Aberdeen's Cabinet who, after some hesitation, accepted office under Palmerston, summed up the situation in his memoirs.

> 1   I had no sympathy with the absurd popular superstition that he was the
>   only man who could conduct the war, or that he could have prevented
>   it. I knew that he had been quite as unforeseeing as any of us as regards
>   all the unexpected contingencies which had led to our difficulties; I
> 5   knew that he had proposed nothing which could have had any effect
>   either in meeting them or preventing them. But ... the popular impres-
>   sion of Palmerston's powers as a War Minister, even although it was
>   largely a delusion, was in itself a qualification for the moment. I was
>   therefore strongly in favour of his forming a Cabinet.

The change of government did not result in any dramatic improvement in the fortunes of the war. Indeed, by April Palmerston was facing a new censure motion, this time in the House of Lords, which was only defeated when he agreed to change some of the administrative personnel running the war. The end of the deadlock came towards the end of 1855, hastened on by the death of the Tsar Nicholas I in March and the accession of the reforming Tsar Alexander II, who wanted to end the war so that he could concentrate on a liberalising domestic programme. Alexander required only the offer of reasonable terms to conclude peace, but Palmerston was now determined upon a tough settlement and believed Russia could be forced to accept one. The war therefore dragged on into 1856 before peace was agreed in March in the Treaty of Paris.

The peace terms were tough but not as severe as Palmerston had intended. He originally hoped to secure a considerable number of territorial concessions from Russia involving many of the Russian gains from Turkey that had been made in and since the Treaty of Kutchuk-Kainardji of 1774, including the return of the Crimea itself to Turkey. Such proposals were unacceptable not only to the Russians but even to many of Palmerston's own colleagues who felt that future conflicts would be rendered inevitable, even if the Russians could be compelled to accept them in the short-term. In the event Russia was forced to accept the effective demilitarisation of the Black Sea (a considerable humiliation for a great power) and also gave up control of the Danube which she had secured at Adrianople in 1828. The position of Turkey was recognised as equal to the other powers and the Sultan acknowledged an obligation of 'generous intentions towards the Christian population of his Empire'. The value of this pledge was obviously dubious, since it was hardly the first time that such an undertaking had been given. However, all the great powers attended the peace conference in Paris and all agreed to respect the independence and territorial integrity of the Turkish Empire.

The Treaty of Paris of 1856 was a considerable turning point in the diplomatic history of nineteenth century Europe. Russian influence and prestige had taken a severe blow. France now re-emerged as the leading continental power. The Eastern Question, far from being solved, was effectively preserved for at least a further generation because of the improved postition of the Turks. The Russians deeply resented the terms of the peace treaty and blamed Britain for the humiliation they had suffered. Thus the Tsar began to cultivate the French as diplomatic allies after 1856, believing that a revival of traditional Anglo-French rivalry was the best hope for Russia to secure a situation in which the Black Sea demilitarisation clauses of the treaty could be reversed. How far this policy might have succeeded was never really tested since the outbreak of the Franco-Prussian War in 1870 gave Russia the opportunity to act unilaterally to repudiate the 'Black Sea Clauses'. Alexander II promised the German Chancellor, Bismarck, Russian neutrality in return for a free hand in the Black Sea. With France embroiled in war and Britain following a more isolationist foreign policy under Gladstone (see page 130) the Russians were able to restore their position in the Black Sea with a simple declaration of intent which was ratified by a conference of the great powers in 1871. With the revival of Russia, the Eastern Question was restored to the forefront of European diplomacy and within a few years would bring Europe to the brink of war once again.

Making notes on 'Britain and the Eastern Question'

Working through this chapter and any other reading you may do on this topic, you need to organise your notes around several key issues which generally form the basis of questions set in examinations.
1. What issues were at stake in the Eastern Question?
a) The nature of the Turkish Empire itself.
b) The strategic implications of the collapse of Turkish rule in south-east Europe and elsewhere.
c) The specific interests of the various great powers.
d)   In what ways did Britain attempt to prop up Turkey?
2. How consistent was British policy on the Eastern Question?
a) What policy did Britain pursue in relation to Russia - how far was it collaborative - how far antagonistic?
b) Did changes in governments or foreign secretaries result in changes in the aims or methods of dealing with the Eastern Question?

Answering essay questions on 'Britain and the Eastern Question'

There are two general categories of questions:
a) The general foreign policy questions which require some refer-
    ence to the Eastern Question in order to achieve a full answer.
    Study the following examples.
1. 'Palmerston's conduct of foreign policy between 1830 and 1851
    was marked by a complete lack of principles and an inconsis-
    tency in approach.' How far do you agree with this verdict?
2. To what extent did British foreign secretaries pursue consistent
    policies in Europe between 1815 and 1865?
    Both these questions would require some consideration of the
    Eastern Question, but, in both cases you would need to be selec-
    tive in your use of that material because it is only one aspect of
    the question. You would need to integrate your references to
    the Eastern Question into a wider discussion of foreign policy.
    The focus of the question 1 is in two parts - first, did Palmerston
    have no principles? - second, was he inconsistent in his
    approach? These are two separate issues and you will need to
    disentangle them and find suitable material to substantiate an
    argument covering each of them. In regard to the Eastern
    Question you will need to make some judgements about
    Palmerston's policies and then deploy those judgements as part
    of your response. For instance, you might decide that the
    Eastern Question offers little in respect of a judgement about
    his principles or lack of them and that there are other areas of
    foreign policy which support an argument on this aspect more
    clearly. You might therefore limit your use of Eastern Question
    material to a consideration of his consistency in approach - was
    he inconsistent in the way he dealt with the Russians, seeming at
    times to be collaborating with them and yet at other times
    clearly attempting to counter their influence? - or, was this only
    an 'apparent' inconsistency which arose out of his pusuit of a
    consistent objective?
b) The more specific type of question, aimed directly at Britain and
    the Eastern Question, might either target a particular event or
    issue or invite a more general assessment of British policy over
    the whole period or a large part of it. Which of the following
    examples fit into each category?
1. Account for the difficulties experienced by Britain in dealing
    with the Greek crisis in the 1820s.
2. To what extent was the Crimean War a necessary exercise to
    protect vital British interests?
3. How far did successive British governments pursue a consistent
    policy towards the Eastern Question between 1815 and 1865?
4. How successful was Palmerston in achieving his objectives in
    regard to the Eastern Question between 1830 and 1856?

Finally consider the following question:
5. To what extent was British foreign policy fundamentally anti-Russian in the period 1815-56?
   This question, in its various forms, is often treated by candidates as an 'Eastern Question' question in disguise. However, while exclusive concentration on the Eastern Question would result in an answer which covered a substantial amount of the relevant material - it would still be perceived as a limited answer because it would leave out important issues such as the Polish Question, the 1848 Revolutions and imperial questions such as India and Afghanistan. You might use this question and those suggested under (a) on the previous page as the basis for an exercise in drawing together material from more than one chapter of this book to integrate into a response to broader questions of this kind.

Source-based Questions on 'Britain and the Eastern Question'

Look at the sources on pages 96 and 98 relating to Britain's declaration of war against Russia in 1854:
a) What arguments does Russell use to justify the declaration of war on Russia. (5 marks)
b) In what ways does Bright directly contradict Russell's arguments? (5 marks)
c) Comparing the two sources, what is the fundamental point of interpretation of the crisis over which Russell and Bright must be presumed to disagree? (5 marks)
d) To what extent do these sources point to differing ideas about ways in which foreign policy should be conducted for the benefit of Britain? (10 marks)

Summary Diagram
Britain and the Eastern Question, 1815-65

1815: Britain recognised Turkish Empire as an essential element in European 'balance of power'

1821-30: Greek Wars of Independence caused friction between the great powers and division of opinion in Britain

Britain and Russia cooperated to try to resolve the crisis in St Petersburg Protocol of 1826

1831-3: First Mehemet Ali Crisis led to Russian intervention as Britain failed to respond to Sultan's plea for help

Treaty of Unkiar Skelessi gave Russia an influence in Turkey that was unacceptable to British interests

---

1839-41: Second Mehemet Ali Crisis resulted in British intervention and Straits Convention of 1841

Palmerston collaborated with Russia against France. New Sultan promised reforms in the Turkish Empire, but little progress was made

---

1844-51: Tsar's visit to London in 1844 resulted in misunderstandings of Britain's view of Eastern Question

In 1848-9 Russian intervention to quell rebellions in Austrian Empire led to the rise of anti-Russian feelings in Britain

---

1851-4: Build up of tension between France and Russia over the 'Holy Places' of Christianity within the Turkish Empire

Britain increasingly feared Russia intended to break up the Turkish Empire

Turkish resistance to Russia led to war and the intervention of Britain and France against Russia

Crimean War 1854-6

1856: Crimean War ended and Palmerston insisted on a penal settlement against Russia including the Black Sea Clauses in the Treaty of Paris

6 The Challenge of Nationalism

Between the 1848 Revolutions and the death of Palmerston in 1865, Britain had to adapt its foreign policy to the reality of two great movements of nationalism in Europe. One of these brought about the unification of the various Italian states into the single nation state of Italy. The other brought the German states under the influence of Prussia and this would lead within a few years of Palmerston's death to the creation of a new German Empire in central Europe.

These two processes affected Britain in different ways. In the case of Italy the most immediate effect was felt in the domestic political arena as the issue of the unification of Italy became a great liberal cause around which radicals and liberals could unite in common agreement - the founding of the Liberal Party in 1859 was significantly connected to this issue. So far as the balance of power was concerned Italy itself, to most intents unified by the early 1860s, was too weak a state to affect the overall diplomatic and strategic balance. However, Italian unification was a process which took place in opposition to the interests of Austria. In order for there to be an Italian nation Austria had to give up actual territory and influence in Italy. The process therefore compromised Austria's status as a great power and was evidence of a decline. The same was true of German unification. Once again it was Austria which in effect had to abdicate authority in favour of Prussia. Austria fought wars to prevent these processes of unification and was defeated in both cases. To Palmerston this all represented a paradox. He generally favoured the idea of liberal and national movements in Europe, provided that constitutionalism did not extend itself into democracy. On the other hand, he saw Austria as an essential balancing factor in the general stability of Europe and did not welcome the Austrian decline. This was particularly the case with the question of German unification because here, unlike Italy, is not a process which, even while Palmerston still lived, looked certain fundamentally to change the balance of power. Unlike Italy, the new German nation threatened to be a powerful force in European affairs. A nation which was large, modernising rapidly, blessed with a resourceful population with resources to exploit - such a nation must inevitably pose a challenge in continental Europe to the dominant positions of France and Russia. The question for Britain was - did this represent a threat to British interests or an opportunity to sponsor some new alignment of forces with which to maintain that peace and stability in Europe which was generally held to be so much in British interests?

1 The Unification of Italy

a) Early Trends in Italian Nationalism, 1815-48

There was no great demand for unity among Italians at the time of the Vienna Settlement. On the contrary, there was considerable hostility within and between different regions. In his memoirs Metternich wrote, 'In Italy provinces are against provinces, towns against towns, families against families, and men against men.' There were certainly real differences between north and south in terms of geography, climate, culture and traditions. The Vienna Settlement reflected the opinion of Metternich that Italy was no more than a 'geographical expression', and that of Castlereagh, who saw Italy as a convenient resource for balancing the stability of Europe by compensating Austria for her losses of influence elsewhere.

The Settlement of 1815 disposed of the various units of Italy as follows (see the map on page 30):

- Lombardy and Venetia in the north-east were both placed under direct Austrian rule and in effect absorbed into the Austrian Empire.
- The Kingdom of Naples and Sicily (sometimes known as the Kingdom of the Two Sicilies) in the south was placed under the absolute monarchy of King Ferdinand who was in effect an Austrian 'puppet', placed in power by the Austrians, with whom he immediately concluded a full treaty of alliance.
- The duchies of Parma, Modena and Tuscany were placed under rulers directly connected to Austria.
- The Papal States in central Italy were restored to His Holiness the Pope.
- The Kingdom of Piedmont (also known as the Kingdom of Sardinia) in the north-west which included Savoy, Nice, Genoa and Sardinia became the only truly independent Italian state, serving as a buffer between France and Austria. It, like Naples, was an absolute monarchy.

Early revolts against this system were not so much directed at greater unity as at misrule within each state. These occurred in Naples in 1820 and in Piedmont in 1821. Both were easily suppressed but both attracted sympathy in Britain as movements for constitutionalism against autocracy. However, at government level Castlereagh maintained that the Austrian sphere of influence must be upheld and gave private support to Metternich. Late in 1830 there were uprisings in the Papal States which were again put down by Austrian troops. This time the British reaction was different. Palmerston took a strictly neutral line so far as actual intervention was concerned, but aside from that he made the general British sympathy for limited liberal constitutionalism very clear. He urged the Austrians not to interfere;

when they did so he urged them to withdraw; he urged the French not to intervene and when they ignored him he urged them to withdraw; he intervened almost constantly with advice to both the Papal Government - urging concessions and an amnesty - and the rebels - urging them to be patient and moderate. His interventions had little effect but were popular with his Whig colleagues in Grey's Ministry and helped him distance himself a little from his Tory background. They were also popular with the public which was decidedly anti-papist.

However, Palmerston had deeper motives in his response to the Italian revolts. His primary objective was to prevent any outbreak of war between France and Austria. Under Castlereagh's policy, Italy was intended to be a balancing counter-weight in the European diplomatic balance - Canning had accepted this principle and Palmerston intended that it should be maintained. Therefore, although he supported the idea of more liberal government within the Italian states, he did not support the idea of any fundamental change in the settlement - he wanted the status quo to remain. In any case, he had to accept that in practice Britain had little power to affect the course of events in Italy. But the maintenance of the status quo had been established as British policy, as had the principle that Britain would express views on Italian issues and would expect to play at least some part in Italian diplomacy, however indirect.

Italy remained relatively quiet for the rest of the 1830s and throughout the years of Peel's administration in the 1840s. However, despite the failure of actual insurrections, under the surface a momentum for unification was slowly gathering. The work of Italian literary giants helped this process forward. The plays of Vittorio Alfieri, who had died in 1803, were still popular and portrayed an image of grandeur and liberty associated with Italian traditions. Giacomo Leopardi's poetry inspired visions of Italian greatness in the past glories of the Roman world. Alessandro Manzoni's historical novel 'I Promessi Sposi' (*The Betrothed Couple*), published in 1825, painted an optimistic picture for Italians. Most important of all was the work of Guiseppe Mazzini (1805-72), who combined the attributes of inspirational writer with visionary orator and the role of soldier-politician. Mazzini carried the message of Italian revival and unification outside Italy in the 1830s. He founded a 'Young Italy' movement and later a 'Young Europe' society. He tried to organise revolts and invasions on several occasions in the 1830s and 1840s. These all ended in failure, but Mazzini was the first Italian clearly to identify a political agenda which had as its objective the political unification of the peninsula. He argued for the end of foreign influence in Italy and the establishment of a unified country based on democratic and republican principles and run by Italians, for Italians.

British governments had no sympathy with the ideas of Mazzini, though his presence in Britain as a political refugee at various times was tolerated. In 1842 letters from him in London to a revolutionary group in Naples were intercepted by the Home Office and the Austrians were informed of a planned insurrection which involved a group within the Austrian Navy in a scheme to overturn the Kingdom of Naples and Sicily. As a result some of the revolutionaries were executed to the fury of the Liberals and radicals in Britain. Radical MPs and even the Whig opposition leaders lambasted Peel's Home Secretary, Sir James Graham, for his decision to expose the plot to the Austrians. However, Palmerston stood aside from the criticism and was conveniently absent from the Commons. Privately he sympathised with Graham and felt that Mazzini had abused his refugee status. He also remained convinced that British interests required continued stability in Italy.

b) The 1848 Revolutions in Italy

In the early months of 1848 there were uprisings and/or new constitutional concessions granted in a number of the Italian states. In January the King of Naples and Sicily was forced by rebels in Palermo to grant a constitution; in Tuscany the Grand Duke had to grant representative government under a new constitution; in March, Piedmont's King Charles Albert granted a new constitution and so did the Pope; also in March, Austrian troops were driven out of Milan in Lombardy and from Venice in Venetia. There was little or no coordination in these uprisings. However, the upheavals led to the Piedmontese King becoming expansionist in his ideas. Charles Albert was influenced by aristocratic liberals in Piedmont who were interested in the possibility of uniting the northern states into a single economic unit. He became determined to annex at least Lombardy from Austria and issued a proclamation at the end of March announcing his country's sympathy with the rebels of both Lombardy and Venetia, following this up by attacking the Austrians in Lombardy. This was the start of a war between Piedmont and Austria which the Austrians were ultimately to win decisively. Later in the year the Pope was forced to flee from Rome and a new republic headed by Mazzini was declared. This revolt was put down in the summer of 1849 by the French whose new President Louis Napoleon saw the opportunity to extend French influence in competition with that of the Austrians. By the end of 1849 there was a virtual restoration of the status quo except that Piedmont had retained its new liberal constitution under a new liberal-minded monarch, Victor Emmanuel II, whose father Charles Albert had abdicated in despair at his defeat by Austria.

In Britain there was unrestrained public acclaim for the Italian rebels and disappointment and anger at their demise. Palmerston was privately worried about the destabilising effect that these events might have on the balance of power in Europe, but he had to tread a delicate balance in his public expression of views. He sounded a note of caution in 1849:

1 Austria is a most important element in the balance of European power,
   a barrier against encroachment on the one side, and against invasion on
   the other. The political independence and liberties of Europe are bound
   up with the maintenance and integrity of Austria as a great European
5 power; and therefore anything which weakens Austria must be something which Englishmen ought to try to prevent.

On the other hand, he played to his new allies the radicals by
observing:

1 For many years the Governments of Europe imagined that they could
   keep down opinion by force of arms, and revolution which was their
   constant dread. We gave an opinion to the contrary effect ... The result
   has proved that if our opinions had been acted upon, great calamities
5 would have been avoided.

Nevertheless, Palmerston gave no support to the Italian revolutionaries and was privately pleased by their eventual defeat.

c) Cavour, Garibaldi and Italian Unification under Piedmontese Leadership, 1848-61

Despite the setbacks of 1848, the Italian states were set on a course
which saw the creation of a unified Italian state by 1861. This
excluded only Venetia, which was taken by force from Austria in 1866,
and Rome itself, which remained under the Pope, supported by
French troops, until 1871. In Britain, Italian affairs became the
biggest external issue in the politics of the 1850s and, indeed, often
took precedence even over internal affairs. By 1859 it was the most
important issue under discussion and became the most significant
cause of the coming together of Whigs, Peelites and radicals to form
the Liberal Party. It was even sufficiently important to Gladstone to
cause him to abandon his hostility towards Palmerston and serve
under him from 1859 until 1865. Once Palmerston declared his
support for the principle of Italian unification, Gladstone felt that he
must overlook Palmerson's other failings.

Why did events in Italy so absorb British politicians? A number of
factors came together to produce this effect. First there was the long-
standing interest of the ruling classes in the world of classical antiq-
uity. Italy was an automatic destination for the educated British trav-
eller. All the leading politicians visited the great sites of Roman
civilisation and most were well-versed in the great Latin texts. Lord
Derby, the leader of the Conservative Party from 1846 until 1868, was
one of the country's great classical scholars - as Disraeli noted bitterly
on more than one occasion, Lord Derby much preferred translating
Greek and Latin texts to politics. Gladstone was another leading

politician with a strong classical interest. He also spoke Italian fluently, and many British aristocrats acquired at least a smattering of the language to facilitate their travels. However, in the 1850s and early 1860s two new elements emerged to draw the attention of all classes in Britain to the Italian scene. One was the emergence of Piedmont as a modernising liberal state under the political leadership of Count Camillo di Cavour, and the other was the dynamic impact of Guiseppe Garibaldi's military campaigns.

Cavour was a Piedmontese aristocrat who had travelled widely in Europe and studied the political systems of Britain and France. He had witnessed the Great Reform Crisis in Britain in 1831-2 at first hand and was particularly impressed by the British political system and by Peel's economic policy in the 1840s, which had reduced taxation on trade and basic necessities. He was especially impressed with the way that Peel had been able to resist the claims of the Chartists for greater political democracy, whilst at the same time delivering policies which benefited all social classes. In 1847 he founded a liberal newspaper *Il Risorgimento* (*The Revival* or *Rebirth*). Cavour was one of those liberal aristocrats who had influenced King Charles Albert towards expansionism in 1848-9. Under the new liberal representative constitution of Piedmont, he rapidly rose in political stature and influence. By 1850 he was in charge of commerce and agriculture and in 1852 he became Prime Minister.

Cavour's policies were popular in Britain, where they attracted great attention. The sort of policies he introduced were exactly to the liking of British Liberals and even Conservatives of the 1850s. By this time Peel's economic policy of freeing trade and encouraging exports by low taxation was accepted even by his former colleagues who had opposed and deserted him over the repeal of the Corn Laws in 1846. Disraeli observed as early as 1847 that economic protection was 'dead and damned'. In 1851 the Conservative leader Lord Derby officially confirmed that Free Trade was now a Conservative Party policy. Cavour's policies included reforms in the army, state administration and the law which opened up access to these professions in ways that many would liked to have seen in Britain. He also pioneered new scientific techniques in agriculture and negotiated trade treaties, as well as encouraging new industries. He opened up opportunities for overseas investors to find outlets for their capital in Piedmont - a policy very much in tune with the wishes of British businessmen whose burgeoning profits in a period which some economic historians have termed 'the mid-Victorian Boom' were causing them to look for new investment opportunities. Just as welcome to British opinion were Cavour's policies limiting the power and influence of the Roman Catholic Church. In 1850 he drafted laws which abolished the ecclesiastical courts. In 1855 many religious orders were abolished, leaving only those which worked in charitable areas such as education and caring for the sick. Finally, Cavour launched ambitious schemes to improve communications in Piedmont and to improve links with other countries. Railways were improved and extended and Genoa was modernised into a great commercial port. In short, Cavour was everything any educated, liberal-minded British citizen of the 1850s could have wished for.

However, Cavour did not focus solely on internal reforms in Piedmont. Expansion was an integral part of his policy. To this end he began actively canvassing the support of both Britain and France for a greater Piedmont. Late in 1855 Piedmont joined in the Crimean War on the side of Britain and France, and sent a small army which campaigned quite successfully in 1856. This helped confirm Piedmont's status as the leading Italian state and also restored confidence after the defeats at the hands of Austria in 1848. Although nothing concrete came of Cavour's attempts to secure acceptance of a greater Piedmont at the Paris Peace Conference in 1856, he had scored a significant diplomatic success. In 1859, he effectively provoked a war with Austria, having first secured a promise of French assistance. In the lead up to this war, Cavour's skilful manoeuvres made Austria appear the aggressor and public support for Piedmont in Britain was almost universal, though there was never any question of actual intervention. There was a General Election in progress at the time and Palmerston used the opportunity of a visit to his Tiverton constituency to make a strongly pro-Italian speech which initiated a reconciliation between himself and Gladstone.

With French aid, Piedmont was able to inflict defeats on the Austrians and the Peace of Villafranca (1859), though a big disappointment at the time, gave a strong stimulus to greater unity. Piedmont took over Lombardy and, although it was to remain officially within the Austrian Empire, Venetia was also to be included in a new all-Italy confederation under the nominal presidency of the Pope. However, Cavour was so disgusted by the settlement that he resigned for a short period in protest. The Peace of Villafranca was opposed in Britain because it seemed to give too much influence to the French and not enough reward to Piedmont. Palmerston was joined in his condemnation of the Treaty by unlikely allies such as Queen Victoria and Gladstone. In practice, the peace provisions were not very well thought out and the arrangements soon collapsed. Other areas, such as Tuscany, wanted to unite with Piedmont and the Pope did not want the presidential role assigned to him. Palmerston, hoping to avoid a resumption of war in Italy, intervened decisively with moral support for Piedmont, the enlargement of which he now saw as necessary to ensure future stability. Palmerston's Foreign Secretary, Lord John Russell, came up with a plan at the beginning of 1860 under which the Italian Duchies could vote through their elected assemblies for union with Piedmont. Cavour, now back in office, concluded a new agreement with the French that Piedmont would cede Savoy and Nice to France in return for a free hand to annex all the Duchies which wished to join Piedmont. Austria had little choice but to agree.

The result was that Piedmont had expanded to cover roughly half the Italian Peninsula - Venetia, Rome and the Kingdom of Naples and Sicily remained independent. Palmerston now hoped that Italian affairs would stabilise but his hopes were soon to be dashed. Guiseppe Garibaldi, an Italian adventurer, who had once been a follower of Mazzini, launched an attack on Naples and Sicily with the objective of incorporating the Kingdom into Piedmont. Privately Palmerston was appalled by this development. Garibaldi was a republican who had once, as a follower of Mazzini, infiltrated the Piedmontese Navy in order to induce it to revolt. He had been condemned to death for his intrigues but had escaped to South America. Garibaldi's republican and democratic sympathies appealed to Cavour no more than they appealed to Palmerston. Cavour was also doubtful about the integration of Naples and Sicily with Piedmont, at least in the short-term, because they were so backward economically and likely to prove a liability rather than an asset to Piedmont. However, neither Cavour nor Palmerston had much choice about this matter. Garibaldi's campaign caught the imagination of liberals all over Europe and especially in Britain where he became a hero overnight. Palmerston was virtually compelled to give moral support to the campaign and late in 1860, Russell issued a famous declaration in which he referred to the right of all states to start revolutions for liberty and spoke of 'the gratifying spectacle of a people building up the edifice of their liberties and consolidating the work of their independence'. Britain's diplomatic support, and British naval power in the Mediterranean, played a crucial part now in convincing Austria and France to stay out of Italian affairs and the new unified state of Italy (excluding Rome and Venetia) was officially proclaimed in March 1861.

Two wars which did not directly involve Italy brought about the completion of the unification process. In 1866, Austria became involved in a war with Prussia. Italy allied itself with the Prussians and, although the Italian military campaign against Austria was unsuccessful, the defeat of Austria by the Prussian army allowed Italy to annex Venetia as part of the Peace Settlement. In 1870, war broke out between France and Prussia and as a result French troops were withdrawn from Rome and the city was occupied by Italian troops. Italy's hold on the historic capital was confirmed by the defeat of the French by the Prussians in 1871.

2 The Unification of Germany

a) The German States, 1815-48

The question of German unification never held the same romantic appeal as that of Italy for the British public, press or politicians. Even amongst radicals the attempts of German nationalists and liberals to secure constitutional change and advance German aspirations to unity seemed to attract relatively limited attention. The Vienna Settlement created a German Confederation of 39 sovereign states which was intended to guarantee the internal and external peace of the region (see the map on page 30). Its proximity to France meant that stability there was essential. From the British viewpoint, therefore, the maintenance of the status quo in Germany was of prime importance, especially as until 1837 the British monarch was also the ruler of the German kingdom of Hanover. This connection was severed in 1837 because Victoria, William IV's successor to the British crown, as a woman, was debarred by Hanoverian law from inheriting the throne. There were outbreaks of unrest in the German states in 1819 which were curbed by Metternich, who persuaded the Prussians to cooperate with Austria in a system of repression which became known as the 'Carlsbad Decrees'. These were routinely condemned in the British press, but Castlereagh gave Metternich his support and encountered little direct pressure in Parliament over the events in Germany. As with other areas of Europe, 1830-32 proved an unsettled period in the German states, but once again British interest was muted, with the focus on the Belgian question attracting the public meetings and providing pressure on politicians. Palmerston, preoccupied with events in Belgium and Italy and then the Middle East, scarcely noted problems in Germany.

b) Germany During the 1848 Revolutions

In March 1848 a revolution broke out in Prussia and a new liberal constitution was proclaimed. However, as with most of the other outbreaks, the process of recovery by the old regime then set in. By the end of the year the Prussian King, Frederick William, had substituted his own more limited constitution, restoring power firmly to the nobility and his own final authority. For a time it looked as if the upheavals of 1848 would lead to the unification of Germany. However, there was a major stumbling block. Was unity to be pursued under Prussian or Austrian auspices? The northern states of Germany were Protestant and tended to look to the Prussians for leadership, whilst the southern states were Roman Catholic and tended to look towards Austria. It was to be expected that Britain would naturally favour Protestantism over Catholicism, but the reality was that British interests were not really served by any confrontation between Prussia and Austria, especially if Austria were to be severely weakened in the process. When the widespread agitation for unification came to nothing, the restoration of the status quo in Germany in 1848-9 therefore suited British interests well.

c) The Process of Unification under Prussia

This process began before 1848 with the formation of a 'Zollverein' or customs union initiated by Prussia as early as 1818. The idea of this was to remove trade barriers between various German states so as to encourage trade and economic development. This system grew so that by 1844 it covered practically all the German states bar Austria and a few small areas such as Hanover. The Zollverein did not begin with the aim of promoting political union but the increased economic interdependence it brought through common taxation policies, commercial and banking connections and road and rail links, had the effect of encouraging closer political ties. The Zollverein came to present a serious threat to the leadership of Austria in the German states. Prussia became economically supreme in the region and began to develop the economic power which supported her emergence as a genuine great power in Europe. The other German states, even the predominantly Roman Catholic ones of the south, became accustomed to regarding Prussia as the leading German state. In Britain the Zollverein was generally welcomed as an encouragement to trade. The process of freeing trade had begun in Britain in the 1780s under William Pitt but had been set back by the French Wars. In the 1820s under William Huskisson at the Board of Trade free trade policies had once again come to the fore. In the 1840s Sir Robert Peel's ministry had taken the first decisive steps through his great budgets of 1842 and 1845 to effectively deregulate trade. The process would be completed by Peel's greatest disciple, Gladstone, in the 1850s and 1860s. The 'economic unification' of Germany under Prussian leadership was therefore very much in tune with the economic ideas which predominated in Britain. There was a rapid increase of trade between Britain and the German states during this period and the start of a pattern of trade which would see the eventually unified German Empire after 1871 become Britain's largest trading partner in the years leading up to the outbreak of the Great War in 1914.

In the 1850s Austria's position deteriorated even more seriously. Its prestige was undermined by the 1848 revolutions which it was only able to suppress with Russian assistance. In 1854-6, during the Crimean War, Austria was painfully indecisive. Fearing to side with Britain and France against the Russians, yet at the same time fearing the probability of a Russian defeat, Austria hesitated and incurred the contempt of both sides. The Russians felt that Austria owed a debt of gratitude to them for the help Russia had provided during the upheavals of 1848-9. Britain and France felt that an Austrian declaration in their favour might have forced the Russians to back down and thus averted the war altogether. In the late 1850s Austria suffered further humiliation at the hands of the French and Piedmontese in the process of Italian unification which was a clear reversal of Austrian interests in a region which was supposed to be a clear area of Austrian influence. Britain moved decisively in favour of Italian unification and Austria was increasingly seen as an archaic and moribund state falling rapidly behind in a modernising, dynamic Europe. In comparison, Prussia seemed to be the very epitome of a modern state with its developing industrial base and improving agriculture.

The final factor which led to German unification under Prussia was the rise to power in Prussia of one of the most dominant figures to emerge in Europe in the nineteenth century, Count Otto von Bismarck. Bismarck was a Prussian supremacist rather than strictly a German nationalist, but in seeking the expansion and supremacy of Prussia he was, in effect, performing the same role. As Prussian Prime Minister from 1862, he concentrated first on securing Prussian dominance in the northern states and prevented the Austrians from belatedly entering the Zollverein. He then sabotaged an Austrian attempt to achieve greater unity with the southern states in 1863 by persuading the Prussian King not to attend the meeting set up by Austria. Without Prussia in attendance the southern German states would not commit themselves to anything and the meeting failed. Britain generally sympathised with Prussia in these developments. Although Bismarck was at heart an authoritarian who despised liberalism and favoured a near autocratic system, this was not really apparent at this stage. German unity was a clear policy of German liberals and Bismarck's policies seemed so clearly to be realising this objective that the true nature of his politics remained unclear. British concern about the growing power of Prussia did not crystallise until Bismarck began to turn towards military methods of achieving his aims and by then it was too late for Britain effectively to intervene.

In 1863, Palmerston became alarmed at the deteriorating relations between Prussia and Denmark. The regions of Schleswig and Holstein had long been a source of conflict between the two countries. In 1848 Prussia and Denmark had even fought a brief war over the future of the area and a compromise, unsatisfactory to both parties, had been hammered out under British mediation in an agreement known as the London Protocol in 1852. In 1863, the Danes announced plans for the incorporation of Schleswig into Denmark and this gave Bismarck grounds to mobilise a general German response in which even the Austrians became involved. Palmerston wanted to see a permanent settlement of the question but could not accept the idea that such a settlement could emerge without Britain being a party to the arrangements. He therefore threw his weight behind the Danes, not particularly because he approved of their position, but because he felt that in this way he was balancing the situation and creating a basis for a negotiated settlement. This was after all the classic manoeuvre, according to Palmerston's thinking, through which Britain could act as the 'arbiter of Europe'. However, Palmerston went so far as to suggest that, if Denmark were attacked, Britain would intervene on the

Danish side. This was unwise. It encouraged the Danes to think that their position was stronger than it really was and made them more intransigent. Bismarck was not bluffed and went ahead with a joint Prussian-Austrian war against Denmark in February 1864. By April the Prussian-Austrian forces were moving into Denmark itself. Palmerston knew full well that direct British intervention was impossible. Quite apart from the strategic problems, there was simply no will to intervene from public opinion, the press or Parliament. In desperation he arranged a conference in London in an attempt to save the Danes. But this was a useless exercise. The Danes, aggrieved at being let down, as they (not unfairly) saw it, by the British, refused to cooperate and the Prussians simply went through the formalities, knowing that the situation was in reality in their hands. Bismarck concluded an agreement with the Austrians under which the sovereignty of Schleswig-Holstein was to be shared between them. This was changed in 1865 into a system whereby Austria administered Holstein while Prussia administered Schleswig. In all these arrangements Britain was able to play no part whatsoever. Palmerston was 80 in 1865 and he died in October of that year a few weeks short of his 81st birthday. He left a situation in which for the first time since 1815 decisions were being made about the future balance of power in Europe without any British input.

Of course, Bismarck had no intention of keeping to his agreement with Austria. Indeed, it has been argued that he had involved the Austrians only as a cover while he prepared to eliminate them from the German equation once and for all. In 1866 he used disagreements over the administration in the two areas as a pretext for a war with Austria in which the Prussia army won a decisive victory at the only major battle, Sadowa, in July 1866. The peace settlement, the Treaty of Prague, was a triumph for Bismarck. The German confederation was dissolved altogether and Prussia absorbed Schleswig-Holstein, Hanover and several other German states. Although there were still some northern states in a separate new confederation, this was clearly under Prussian control. Similarly the southern states, still nominally independent, were recognised as under Prussian leadership. The stage was set for Bismarck's momentous and victorious confrontation with France in 1870 which became one of the landmark events of nineteenth century European history and is discussed from a British point of view in Robert Pearce's Access to History volume, *Britain and the European Powers, 1865-1914*.

The process of German unification was notable for the lack of a British contribution. Although Britain had not intervened directly in the events which brought about the unification of Italy, British diplomacy had been a constant factor and British naval power in the Mediterranean had been pivotal in determining the response of France and Austria in the 1860-61 campaigns of Garibaldi. There was no comparable situation over the future of Germany. On the contrary, Palmerston's abortive attempt to intervene in the Schleswig-Holstein crisis in 1863-4 only served to highlight how impotent Britain was in that situation. There was no real agreement in Britain, in any case, about the rights and wrongs of German unification. In some quarters the rise of Prussia was beginning to be seen as a real change in the balance of power in Europe, though whether or not this would favour British interests was still unclear. However, others argued that the rise of Prussia was a stabilising factor which would limit both the French and the Russians in the future and assist the long-term British policy of preserving peace in Europe.

3 To What Extent Did the Rise of Nationalism in Europe Present Problems for Britain?

This question can be answered by classifying the problems into two categories.

a) Internal Affairs

In domestic terms the rise of nationalism, as exemplified most obviously by events in Italy and Germany, presented only one clear parallel, but it was an important one - Ireland. The nature of British government in Ireland was a source of embarrassment to British Liberals. Many people thought that it seemed to match or even exceed in oppressiveness anything which the most despotic of continental autocrats could achieve. Early in the next century the Irish leader John Redmond, looking back at just over a century of British administrative failure since the Act of Union in 1800 characterised it thus:

1 Take the test of population. While in every civilised country in Europe
   the population has increased ... in Ireland it has diminished by one half.
   Take the test of civil liberty. There has been a coercion act for every year
   since the Union was passed ... which enables the Lord-Leiutenant, at his
5 arbitrary discretion, by the stroke of the pen, to suspend trial by jury,
   personal liberty, freedom of discussion and the right of public meeting
   ... There have been since the Union three insurrections, all of them
   suppressed in blood, with sacrifices untold in the prison cell and upon
   the scaffold ... Take the test of the prosperity of Ireland ... it is the
10 history of constantly recurring famines every few years over a large
   portion of the west and north-west of the country. Take the test of
   industrial development. A history of industries deliberately suppressed
   by British Acts of Parliament, and not one finger lifted in the last
   hundred years to advance industrial prosperity ...

Such a record was already clearly in place by the middle years of the nineteenth century. The great famine of 1845-50 had killed around a

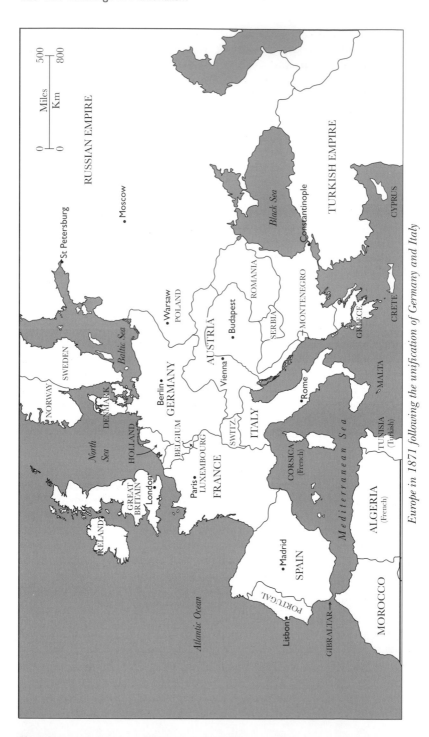

Europe in 1871 following the unification of Germany and Italy

million Irish people and forced a further two million to emigrate. Whig and Tory governments alike had stood firm against any change in the constitutional relationship between Great Britain and Ireland and both had made free with coercion acts. International attention had already focused on the incompatibility of British statesmen's criticism of the internal policies of European rulers with their own attitude to nationalist aspirations in Ireland. By 1865 the underground nationalist organisation known as the Fenians had extensive networks of members in Ireland and on the British mainland as well as in the United States. It was modelled to some extent on the secret nationalist societies of Europe which extreme Irish nationalists had encountered on the Continent whilst seeking refuge from arrest. It was this state of affairs and the great blot on the record of enlightened British government which Ireland represented which led the great Liberal leader, Gladstone, to proclaim upon becoming Prime Minister in 1868 that his mission was to 'pacify Ireland'.

The uncomfortable parallels which might be drawn between continental despotism and British rule in Ireland did nothing whatever to dampen enthusiasm for liberal and nationalist movements in Europe amongst the British public and the British press, both of which were conveniently blind to such considerations. It was less easy for politicians to take this line since they had to face the possible consequences of successful nationalist campaigns on the continent stirring up entirely unwelcome imitative movements in Ireland. They also had to deal with the barbs which from time to time came through diplomatic channels. Palmerston's basic suspicion of nationalist movements was to some extent related to his Irish connection - he was, after all, an 'Irish' landlord. It was part of the British case against the idea that Ireland was in fact a nation, to argue that the various regions of Ireland were so dissimilar in nature that any kind of separate autonomy for Ireland was pointless. This was an argument which was seriously undermined by the processes of unification in Italy and Germany.

b) External Affairs

There was some limited parallel with European nationalism for Britain in terms of the British Empire, but generally speaking the idea that nationalism in Europe was equatable with nationalist aspirations amongst colonial, let alone native, populations simply did not occur to people. The colonial settlers from Britain were seen as, and overwhelmingly saw themselves as, still British. It was true that in the eighteenth century Britain had lost the American colonies to nationalist feelings of a kind, but by the 1850s this was far in the past and was seen as the consequence not of nationalism as such but as resulting from the awkwardness of the Americans and the limitations of the British political system at that time, which had allowed insufficient representation to the settlers. The idea that white settlers had a right to a reasonable degree of internal self-government was already established in the Cape, in Canada and in the Australian colonies. In India the mutiny of 1857 shocked and angered public opinion, but the idea that it might represent some legitimate native aspiration for independence was seen as ludicrous in a society in which the racial supremacy of Europeans and especially the English was taken as a self-evident truth.

More important, however, was the impact of nationalism on the balance of power in Europe. Here matters were more difficult. Public opinion, either led or followed by the press according to circumstances, was almost wholly and uncritically in favour of nationalist uprisings. These were generally seen as evidence of how unfit European powers were to rule their subject peoples. But at government level it was seen as being more complex. Generally speaking Whig/Liberal administrations had a higher natural threshold of sympathy for nationalist movements than did their Tory/Conservative counterparts. Even so it could not be denied that nationalism posed a threat to the established balance of power in Europe. If the status of empires was to change and they were to diminish or grow stronger, if new countries altogether were to take shape with their own aspirations and potential for the future, then this was bound to have a destabilising effect, at least in the short term. Palmerston, as we have seen, had no great affection for nationalism, despite his playing to the press and radical opinion. He judged Italian unification purely on the practical ground of whether it affected British interests. He actually wanted to see Austria give up its Italian territory and influence, but this was not because he saw it as basically illegitimate, but because he believed that the Italian connection made Austria weaker and more vulnerable. He wrote in 1848 that Italy was for Austria 'the heel of Achilles and not the shield of Ajax'. He wanted Austria to survive as a great power in Europe. He did not particularly want a united Italy. The same was true in the case of Germany. In old age, shortly before his death, he consoled himself over the humiliation he had suffered in respect of the Danish crisis of 1864, by observing that 'it is desirable that Germany, in the aggregate, should be strong, in order to control those two ambitious and aggressive powers, France and Russia, that press upon her west and east'. This was a sentiment which would have been recognisable and acceptable to Castlereagh and Wellington and would not have caused disquiet to any of the directors of British foreign policy who had come after them.

The events in Germany and Italy from 1848 to 1865 demonstrated that Britain was in effect the last power to see the 1815 settlement as still providing the basis for European stability. Events in 1863-4 especially - verbal encouragement to the Danes unaccompanied by material help - showed that in future Britain would either have to be prepared to do more in European affairs in a direct way or be prepared to say less. The idea that Britain had some superior moral right to be the arbiter of Europe was based on the credit and credibility accumulated in the era of Pitt, Wellington and Castlereagh. This was a line of credit upon which Palmerston had drawn heavily in the long years of his control of foreign policy and it was a credit reserve which was pretty well exhausted by 1865. The fact was that the processes of Italian and German unification had taken place in the relative absence of British influence or control - more so in the case of Germany than in the case of Italy, where Britain had at least been more evident. But there was no disguising the fact that the process even there did not depend on Britain's views.

By 1865 there were clear grounds for concern about the ability of Britain to secure her interests in relation to events in Europe. There was a new pattern of power relationships emerging in which Britain would need to find a place. In 1864 the future Lord Salisbury (then still known as Lord Robert Cecil), the man who would one day dominate British politics and British foreign policy even more completely than Palmerston had done, reflected in an article in the conservative *Quarterly Review* on the low ebb of British influence in Europe:

1 We have been taught to believe that England's voice is of weight in the councils of the world. Our national pride has been fed by histories of the glorious deeds of our fathers, when single-handed they defied the conqueror to whom every other European nation had been compelled
5 to humble itself. Resting upon these great deeds of past days, we have borne ourselves proudly in our dealings with other countries, speaking in the tone of those who have proved by action the weight and significance of their words. Until recently the rank we have thus assumed has been accorded to us readily ... Those who remembered the Great War
10 [against Napoleon] refused to believe that England could not make good her threats or her promises if she thought fit ... But this condition of things has lamentably changed ... an entire revolution has taken place in the tone of foreign thought in regard to the position of England. Her influence in the councils of Europe has passed away ... Our courage is
15 not only disbelieved, but it is ridiculed as an imposture that has been found out ... Our critics abroad are mistaken in believing that the character of the English peopled is changed from what it was ... and yet it is not the less true that our policy has really borne the character which has been affixed to it abroad. It has been essentially a policy of
20 cowardice. This word is often loosely used, and ... may only be the imputation with which an opponent tries to blacken a policy of moderation ... But a policy of moderation and a policy of cowardice ... are in reality easily distinguished ... cowardice ... is applicable to a policy which, according to the power of the opponent, is either valiant or
25 submissive - which is dashing, exacting, dauntless to the weak and timid and cringing to the strong ...

The challenge of nationalism in Europe revealed that Britain had for the time being at least become a spectator in European affairs - diplomatically bankrupt and suspected of cowardly posturing - it would be more than a decade into the future before Disraeli and Salisbury would restore British credibility at the Congress of Berlin in 1878.

Making notes on 'The Challenge of Nationalism'

It would be fairly unusual to find a question at 'A' level which focused *exclusively* on the issues raised for Britain by nationalism in Europe. The purpose of this chapter has been to provide a wider context for consideration of British policy in relation to Europe - to form part of the ideas and evidence which could be deployed when answering a more general question.

You can therefore concentrate on a few limited themes:

1. What factors caused British governments to have doubts about the effects of nationalist campaigns in Europe?
2. Were British governments able to develop any consistent principles to apply in relation to nationalism in Europe?
3. Make a list of points where Britain tried to affect the course of events in Italian and German affairs. Indicate whether these attempts were successes or failures.
4. Given that British diplomatic credibility was low in Europe by 1865, how important had the processes of Italian and German unification been in bringing this about? To determine this will obviously require reference to other chapters.

Source-based question on 'The Challenge of Nationalism'

1. Britain's Standing in Europe in 1864

Read the extract from Lord Robert Cecil's article of 1864 on page 123 and answer the following questions.

a) Who was, in your opinion, the primary target of Lord Robert Cecil's criticism in this article? (5 marks)
b) What does Cecil see has having been the basis of British (English) influence in the past? (5 marks)
c) How far would you agree that, when this article was written, recent British policy had been based on cowardice? (10 marks)

Summary Diagram

The Challenge of Nationalism

1815: Treaty of Vienna largely ignored nationalities in favour of stability and the interests of the great powers

---

1819-20: Revolts in Italy and unrest in the German states led to Austrian intervention on behalf of the status quo. Britain gave diplomatic support to Austria

---

1830-48: A gradual increasing of interest in national and liberal ideas in both Italy and Germany. German Zollverein increased sense of German national identity. Development of Italian *Risorgimento*

1848: Revolutions all over Europe - most were suppressed (apart from in France) but in Italy resulted in the rise of Piedmont and the weakening of Austrian influence. Austrian prestige was also reduced in German states with Prussia emerging as the leading power. Palmerston offered qualified support for liberal movements but reiterated the importance of Austria to European stability

---

1848-65: Piedmont moves closer to France. This resulted in an alliance with France (1859), war with Austria and finally the Peace of Villafranca (1859). Palmerston supported the principle of Italian unification, uniting liberal opinion in the formation of a 'Liberal Party'. Garibaldi's 1860-1 campaign led to the creation of the Kingdom of Italy. Rise of Prussia under Bismarck led to the expansion of Prussian State and the weakening of Austria. Prussian war against Denmark showed the weakness of British position in 1864.

Stage was set for creation of a German Empire (1871) and completion of Italian unity in 1866 (Venetia) and 1871 (Rome)

7 Conclusion: The Conduct and Principles of British Foreign Policy, 1815-65

1 Castlereagh and Canning

Castlereagh's biographer, C.J. Bartlett, argued that there was a 'New Diplomacy' involved in the way Castlereagh conducted British foreign policy with regard to European affairs. Bartlett justified this partly by pointing out that Castlereagh himself saw his diplomacy as representing a very different approach to that which had been adopted in the eighteenth century. To Castlereagh the 'old diplomacy' was characterised by intrigues and short-sighted jostling for advantage, and had 'poisoned the public health of the body politic of Europe'. According to Castlereagh, these destructive approaches had 'happily in latter years been in great measure banished, at least from the councils of the Quadruple Alliance'. However, Bartlett accepted that Castlereagh's conduct of policy was a peculiarly personal one, 'the most personal ever pursued by a British Foreign Secretary'. It was based on his personal relationship with foreign statesmen and rulers and it could not have been adopted by his successor Canning even if he had wanted to - which he did not - because he did not have Castlereagh's prestige and was not trusted, most noticeably, by Metternich.

The death of Castlereagh, just before the Vienna-Verona meetings in 1822, clearly illustrates both the strengths and the weaknesses of his methods. Had he lived, the discussions might have resulted in Britain, Austria, and Russia working together over the Greek crisis and reaching agreement over wider matters, including Spanish America. However, Metternich only had faith in Britain as long as Castlereagh was in control of policy. Equally, Castlereagh relied heavily on the reciprocal effect of his relationships. Had Metternich died or lost office or if the Tsar had died, all his planning would have been at risk. Canning was bound by no such considerations. Where his predecessor had aimed to find a European basis for settling the problem of the future of the Spanish American colonies, he acted unilaterally, although he invoked a largely illusory concept of Anglo-American co-operation to cover up this fact. With the Russians, he could make no progress while Alexander lived but, once he was dead (1825), he approached the new Tsar directly and without attempting to develop the concerted European approach for which Castlereagh would have instinctively striven. Canning was not interested in developing allied responses to potential international problems before they arose; he preferred to devise strategies to cope with situations as they occurred, acting either unilaterally if necessary, or with whichever party seemed appropriate or feasible in each case. However, this did not mean that he was in any sense isolationist or zenophobic. As his biographer, Wendy Hinde, observed, 'Canning believed passionately in England's greatness, but he did not think she could or should stand isolated and alone'.

The respective merits of Castlereagh and Canning were extensively debated in the 1920s and 1930s by two giants of British diplomatic history, Professors Webster and Temperley. Webster lauded the diplomatic skills of Castlereagh, seen at their best, he argued, in the question of Spanish America. Temperley, on the other hand, advanced the claims of Canning, with his apparent virtues of liberalism and constitutionalism. It was a fascinating academic wrangle but its main long-term effect seems to have been to convince most subsequent writers that the differences between Canning and Castlereagh had been over-stressed, at least in terms of their overall aims, if not in terms of their methods and personalities. In other words, just as Castlereagh's supposed preference for absolutism was a misleading generalisation, so too was Canning's reputation for liberalism. Both were disciples of Pitt and both would have claimed to be basing their aims and methods in foreign policy on principles which he had laid down.

A generation or so after his death, Canning had become a revered figure and his handling of foreign policy came to be seen as a model by politicians of very different temperaments and approaches. Palmerston, Aberdeen, Peel, Disraeli and Gladstone all referred at times to Canning and invoked his memory in reverential tones. However, during his tenure of office there were regular doubts expressed about his conduct of policy. Wendy Hinde has suggested that Canning only survived at all as Foreign Secretary because of the loyal support of Lord Liverpool. George IV hated Canning because of the latter's adherence to the Queen during the great divorce scandal and once expressed the view that Canning was no more capable of conducting foreign policy than a baby. There were other, less prejudiced, critics. Wellington had championed the appointment of Canning to the Foreign Office and indeed it was largely due to the influence of the Duke that Liverpool was able to persuade the very reluctant King to accept him. Before long, however, Wellington grew alarmed at Canning's approach. The latter's blatant efforts to popularise foreign policy, the openness (and regularity) of his public speeches, and his unprecedented habit of publishing large amounts of diplomatic correspondence all caused anxiety to the more conservative-minded elements in the Cabinet. It was a matter of style and temperament more than political philosophy, but it convinced contemporaries, critics and admirers alike, that Canning had brought about some substantive change in the conduct of affairs.

2 Palmerston and Aberdeen

The contrasts between Canning and Castlereagh were to some extent replicated in a later generation by the conflicting personalities and policies of Palmerston and Aberdeen. Where Palmerston was open and flamboyant, Aberdeen was shy and retiring; where Palmerston was thick-skinned and rarely took criticism to heart or held a grudge, Aberdeen was sensitive and insecure. Palmerston outdid even Canning in the mass publication of diplomatic documents and even resorted to publishing articles in the press. Aberdeen despised and distrusted such methods. He was also a poor speaker compared with Palmerston. However, these differences of personality were not the limit of the divergences. Whereas it is reasonable to argue that the differences in approach between Canning and Castlereagh were fairly minimal in terms of policy, this would not be a tenable position to take in relation to Palmerston and Aberdeen.

Palmerston's basic approach to foreign relations was nationalistic. That is not to say that he, any more than Canning, was zenophobic, but rather that he operated on the sole principle of seeking British advantage in any given situation. Aberdeen was fundamentally more internationalist in outlook. Moreover, whereas Palmerston, though not in any sense a warmonger, wanted to avoid war for practical reasons, Aberdeen felt a deep moral aversion to war that went to the very roots of his character. This aversion to war left him far more willing than Palmerston ever was to consider the viewpoints of other countries. It was not that Palmerston could not see or understand the attitudes of others - he simply did not conceive that it was any business of his to consider them except insofar as they might affect his own intentions for the advancement of British interests. Similarly, when it came to preparations for war or using the threat of war, Palmerston had no compunction about using either as a valid lever to get what he wanted. To Aberdeen, the doctrine of preparing for war to ensure peace was an immoral concept - to Palmerston it was commonsense so long as it worked.

3 The 'Schools' of Foreign Policy

R.T. Shannon, in his biography of Gladstone, pointed out that British foreign policy in this period was characterised by three, initially separate and competing traditions or 'schools' of thought.

a) The Palmerstonian School

The theory behind this idea is that Palmerston developed a distinctive approach to the conduct of foreign policy which was based on a combination of Whig/Liberal ideas of constitutionalism deriving from the era of the Vienna Settlement and nationalist concepts which developed in the 1830s and 1840s. This rests on seeing Castlereagh and Canning as representing fundamentally different values in foreign policy. Castlereagh represents a more internationalist approach, while Canning emphasises more nationalist values. Palmerston, who after all became Foreign Secretary as a Canningite Tory in Grey's coalition ministry in 1830, is seen as carrying on the Canning tradition. This involved a basic sympathy with the aspirations of constitutionalists in Europe combined with a rather conservative emphasis on collaboration with Russia and suspicion of France. Initially, this led to clashes with his Whig colleagues in the coalition since they tended to approach foreign questions from the reverse angle - they sympathised with France and detested Russia as a tyrannical autocracy. Gradually however, it is claimed, Palmerston began to incorporate more 'Whiggish' thinking into his policy. After the 1848 revolutions in Europe he increasingly became identified with an anti-Russian approach, and was seen as a champion of Liberal values by the radicals. As suggested above, Palmerston incorporated an aggressive style into his approach with an emphasis on ends rather than means, and on the primacy of British interests above all else.

b) The Aberdonian School

This school is seen as representing a more internationalist approach than that of Palmerston. The idea here is that Lord Aberdeen took up the policies of Castlereagh and emphasised a policy less confrontational and aggressive: one based more on collaboration with other powers and the search for consensus through the concept of the 'Concert of Europe'. Aberdeen had been closely associated with Castlereagh in his early career. He continued to show Castlereagh's influence when he was Foreign Secretary first under Wellington and then under Peel. This separated him from Canning and the Canningites such as Palmerston. Aberdeen's aversion to war is said to have led him towards a very cautious approach to foreign policy which found no place for the brinkmanship of Palmerston. Aberdeen was Foreign Secretary in Peel's administrations between 1841 and 1846 and Peel himself is identified with this approach.

c) The Manchester School

This school is said to derive from the influence of Richard Cobden and John Bright through the Anti-Corn Law League which had it headquarters in Manchester. The League flourished from its foundation in 1839 until the Repeal of the Corn Laws by Peel in 1846. The League in general, and Cobden and Bright as its leaders in particular, were prominent in promoting the idea that there would be substantial benefits to international relations resulting from free trade amongst nations. Cobden, in particular, argued that war was almost always traceable to some economic conflict. Therefore, it followed that to remove conflict from international trade would usher in a new period of peace and prosperity for all mankind. Cobden and Bright regarded war with horror not just on moral grounds (Bright after all was a Quaker), but also because of the waste of money and resources which it involved. War closed markets and ruined trade. The Manchester school therefore advocated trade agreements with other countries but wanted to avoid alliances or 'entanglements' which might draw Britain unwittingly into a conflict

4 Britain as Moral Leader or Arbiter of Europe

It is important to note that all of these traditions or 'schools' were based on an assumption of British moral superiority. Even Cobden and Bright assumed that Britain had to demonstrate moral leadership for the benefit of other nations. Nor was Palmerston so entirely without moral principles as may be thought. In his dealings with other countries in matters of trade and commerce he never sought exceptional privileges for Britain over other nations - only for equal opportunities for all nations. He assumed that British superiority in manufacturing would enable British traders to defeat any competition provided that they faced fair and equal conditions. Whilst this might seem dubious morally in twentieth-century terms, in the context of nineteenth century perspectives it was as moral an approach as can be expected. Moreover, Palmerston was a stickler for international law and was always most reluctant to put himself in the position of having acted illegally. He routinely sought legal advice before taking action and, having received it, he framed his subsequent policies around the need to observe it. Towards the end of this period Gladstone, the politician who was emerging as the most dominant figure for the next generation, began to develop his own approach to foreign policy based on a kind of synthesis of the Aberdonian and Manchester schools. Gladstone gave a high priority to the avoidance of conflict and achieving consensus in international relations. He too proceeded on the assumption that Britain's role (or even duty) was to provide moral leadership and set an example in terms of respecting the rights of other nations and peoples. In other words, although there were differences of opinion about how policy should be conducted and even sometimes about what the actual aims of British foreign policy should be, the basic principle that Britain was set above other nations and had a unique precedence and position in international affairs was accepted almost universally as an obvious and unquestionable reality on which Britain's relationships with the European powers had logically to be based. God had favoured Britain by conferring economic strength on it beyond that of any other power - that blessing was a confirmation of moral superiority and an indication of the moral right of Britain to regard itself as setting a standard to which other nations might aspire.

Working on 'The conduct and principles of British Foreign Policy, 1815-65'

It is more important with this chapter to ensure that you have a clear grasp of the range of views which can be adopted about foreign policy than to compile detailed notes. Try to form an opinion about the various interpretations described. You will need to use other chapters to help you substantiate the conclusions you reach.

Think about and then discuss or write brief notes in response to the following questions:

1. What are a) the similarities, and b) the differences between Castlereagh and Canning as foreign secretaries. Which are the more significant?
2. How do you rate Palmerston as a foreign secretary? Disraeli once described him as 'Ginger Beer rather than Champagne'. What do you think he meant by this, and would you agree with him?
3. Which of the three schools of foreign policy described in this chapter would have served British interests best if implemented consistently between 1815 and 1865?

Answering an essay question under examination conditions

The purpose of this section is to provide an operational model for exam essays by working through an example of a typical examination essay question which might be set on subject matter covered by this book and look at the possible approaches which could be adopted in response. The response itself is a process which ought to involve two stages - a PLANNING stage and an EXECUTION stage. The second stage is, of course, obligatory if you are going to produce any answer at all. However, the first stage is entirely optional, at least in terms of how formally and thoroughly it is undertaken, and many students, whatever their good intentions, either omit or rush their planning, once inside the examination room. The crucial nature of planning answers to essay questions cannot be stressed too strongly and it is to that phase of the process that primary attention is directed here.

Remember that the timing of a standard three-hour History examination, requiring four questions to be attempted, means that a theoretical allocation of 45 minutes is available to deal with each essay answer. However, IN PRACTICE you will need time to read through the paper to identify the questions you wish to tackle. It follows therefore that you cannot allocate a full 45 minutes to every answer and it is wise to PREPARE on the assumption of 40 minutes per essay - this will train you to think and write more quickly and take the pressure off you in the actual examination. Obviously the figures will be different if the examination you are preparing to sit is of a different length, or if the number of questions you are required to answer is not four, but the principles will remain the same.

How should you use the time in practice available to answer each question? It is important to realise that even relatively slow writers can actually write a considerable amount, even in 30 minutes of continuous writing. And if you invest time in the planning stage, that preparation can actually save you time as you execute the answer, so you will be able to write even more. Properly done (and properly used), the plan will also direct your answer more accurately at the target of the question, avoiding that frequent fault of which examiners complain, a lack of RELEVANCE in the answer. Aim therefore to spend at least 5 minutes planning your answer.

Suppose the essay question you have chosen is:

'To what extent were the European revolutions of 1848-9 a turning point at which a conflict between Britain and Russia became inevitable?'

The first step of planning is to UNDERSTAND the question. You need to understand it both LITERALLY and HISTORICALLY (i.e. know what the actual words mean and how the question makes sense as a historical issue). Clearly if you have any problems at this point you must seriously reconsider whether to proceed. This may sound absurdly obvious but marking exam papers shows only too clearly that some students DO start to answer questions which they have not fully considered or understood. Assuming there are no such problems you then proceed to analyse the question as a whole and break it down into the KEYWORDS AND PHRASES. Some people think that it is a good idea to write out the title so that you can circle the keywords etc. as you identify them but, of course, you could do this on the examination paper itself. An analysis of the above title would throw up the following:

TO WHAT EXENT - these words tell you what kind of answer is required. You need to measure or assess the validity of the central idea in the question so as to produce an EVALUATION of that idea. Remember the idea of MEASUREMENT in this type of question - which could easily be worded 'How far …' etc. As an exercise see how many different ways you could reword this question whilst still retaining the evaluative target. Doing this will help you correctly identify an evaluation-type question however it is worded in the examination you sit. You will need to make a SERIES OF JUDGEMENTS about the historical events and issues which the question raises in order to frame your answer.

TURNING POINT - terms like this can sometimes confuse and, however obvious they may seem, they may need some definition in your plan or even in the answer itself. In this case the implication is that the events specified (the 1848 revolutions) caused the future course of events to be different to that which would have occurred had the events never taken place. This leads to the obvious HYPOTHESIS - supposing that there had been no 1848 revolutions, would there still have been a war between Britain and Russia anyway?

INEVITABLE - this is a loaded term in the historical context and must always be examined wherever it occurs. The assumption here is that the war could not have been avoided - it need not necessarily have occurred in 1854 (N.B. The question does not specify 1854), but it must have come at some point. This makes the proposition absolute and many historians would reject the idea of 'inevitability' in almost any context. You do not have to do this, but you should come to some decision about how you are going to respond to this concept.

The rest of the question points you towards the factual content which you will need to consider - The nature of Anglo-Russian relations before 1848 - What exactly happened in 1848-9 to affect how Russia was perceived - The events which followed the 1848 revolutions and how far they were directly related to what happened in 1848-9. You should be able to identify some key events which must be considered. The Anglo-Russian approach to the Greek Question, the First and Second Mehemet Ali Crises, and the circumstances in the Cabinet at the end of 1853 and early 1854, are some examples. At this point your plan is maturing and by this time (if not earlier) you MUST be clarifying in your own mind what will be the argument you will put forward in response. Here are some possibilities for this essay:

1. War between Britain and Russia was never inevitable and the Russian actions in response to the 1848 revolutions could not make it so. You will need to expand on this by developing an alternative argument. This MIGHT be along the lines that, although the Russian response could not make war inevitable, it did make it more LIKELY that Britain and Russia would find themselves clashing in any crisis situation in the future because of the suspicion and public hostility towards Russia in Britain which resulted.

2. You could argue that war between Britain and Russia was inevitable but that it was not the 1848 revolutions which were fundamentally to blame for this. Again you would then expand the lines of the argument to show that other factors were more important in bringing this situation about. To support this idea you would need to show that British policy had long been based on anti-Russian principles and that even when Britain cooperated with Russia the underlying aim was always to curtail Russian expansion.

3. You could argue that war was inevitable between Britain and Russia and that the events of 1848-9 WERE mainly responsible for this situation. Again the argument would need to be developed by showing how relations were changed by British reactions to Russian intervention.

In every case the issue of a 'turning point' needs to be prominent in the discussion and a hypothesis can be deployed to add weight to your arguments. Most crucially of all, you must make your viewpoint clear FROM THE OUTSET. You must NEVER use the essay itself as a fact-finding exercise designed to help you make up your mind about what the answer should be. Students who do this would typically produce an essay which relates the events from 1848 and ends with some variation on the theme 'As can be seen from the above, by 1854 war between Britain and Russia might be considered inevitable but then again ...'. This kind of answer is more or less saying to the examiner - here are all the facts - you make up your own mind about it. Even if the final judgement IS decisive, the points leading up to it are unlikely to be very convincingly arrayed in support of it because they were not put forward specifically for that purpose. By the time you are ready to execute the answer you must know what it is you are going to argue; ideally you should decide this after making your initial assessment of the question. That way the plan itself will be even more effective as an instrument for a successful answer.

Finally some points on EXECUTION:

1. Once you have your plan USE IT - it will help you remain relevant to the question. Some students complete the plan and then never look at it again in the course of writing the essay. Doing this is likely to lead to them making good points in their plan which never actually appear in their answer. Would anybody draw up plans for the building of a house and then never look at them again during the actual construction? If ideas occur to you during the execution of the answer, which you had not thought of during the planning - make an addition to your plan (unless you can use the idea or fact immediately) - this is much better than trying to hang on to it in your memory until it can be properly used, or using it artificially where it has no real purpose, rather than risk forgetting it.

2. Take care in the construction of your sentences. Try not to make them over-elaborate or complex. Quality of language is a factor in examinations at all levels, and poor spelling, poor grammar, poor use of punctuation and lack of clarity in expression can all limit your marks.

3. Avoid excessive scene-setting. Examiners tend to wince when faced with an introduction which reads something like 'before I can answer this question I will have to explain what had happened for a lengthy period prior to these events'. What happened before may well be significant and could no doubt be selectively deployed in a relevant way but it is far better to start with some clear and relevant comment which directly addresses the central theme of the question.

Chronological Table

1812 Castlereagh became Foreign Secretary. Treaty of Chaumont set down the main guidelines for terms of an eventual peace settlement with France. Napoleon's disastrous retreat from Moscow started the process of disintegration of his Empire.

1813 Battle of Leipzig swung the initiative firmly towards the coalition powers. Wellington pushed French forces to the brink of expulsion from Spain.

1814 Surrender of Napoleon and the First Treaty of Paris which imposed relatively lenient terms on France. Napoleon exiled to Elba.

1815 Congress of Vienna. Return of Napoleon. Allied victory at Waterloo. Second Treaty of Paris imposed tougher terms on France. Napoleon exiled to St Helena. Signing of the Holy Alliance and Quadruple Alliance.

1818 Congress of Aix-la-Chapelle brought France back into European diplomatic system.

1820 Revolutions in Spain and Italy. Castlereagh produced the 'State Paper'. Congress of Troppau revealed breach between Britain and the other European great powers.

1821 Start of the Greek Revolt. Congress of Laibach.

1822 Death of Castlereagh. Canning became Foreign Secretary. Congress of Verona.

1823 French intervention in Spain to restore absolute monarchy despite British objections.

1824 Canning recognised independence of former colonies in South America - policy extended in 1825.

1826 Canning reached agreement with Russia (St Petersburg Protocol) over the Greek Question. Britain sent military and naval support to Portugal.

1827 Treaty of London ratified St Petersburg Protocol. Death of Canning. Battle of Navarino: Britain, France and Russia intervened against Turkey on behalf of the Greeks.

1829 Treaty of Adrianople between Russia and Turkey created fears of Russia's future intentions.

1828 Aberdeen became Foreign Secretary. War broke out between Russia and Turkey.

1830 Revolution in France ended the Bourbon monarchy. Belgian Crisis began. Palmerston became Foreign Secretary.

1831 First Mehemet Ali Crisis. Britain failed to respond to Turkish pleas for assistance. Russia saved Turkey from complete defeat by Egyptian forces.

1832 Britain and France collaborated over the Belgian Crisis.

1833 Treaty of Unkiar-Skelessi between Russia and Turkey - very much in Russia's favour.

1834 Palmerston sponsored a new Quadruple Alliance with Spain,

Portugal and France to defend constitutional monarchies in Spain and Portugal.

1839 Second Mehemet Ali Crisis gave Palmerston the chance to undo the Treaty of Unkiar Skelessi. Treaty of London finally resolved Belgian Question with all the great powers agreeing to respect the future neutrality of Belgium.

1841 The 'Straits Convention' revoked the Treaty of Unkiar-Skelessi as the powers agreed in London to maintain Turkish integrity. Aberdeen became Foreign Secretary.

1844 Tsar's visit to London initiated confusion over the Eastern Question.

1846 Palmerston returned as Foreign Secretary. Tension rose between Palmerston and Queen Victoria over the conduct of foreign policy.

1848 Revolutions all over Europe. Palmerston remained officially neutral but indicated a general sympathy with constitutionalism.

1849 Russian intervention in Austrian Empire to put down revolts inflamed British public opinion.

1850 Don Pacifico debate. Visit of General Haynau to London provoked a diplomatic incident.

1851 Kossuth's visit to London created further tension between Palmerston and the Queen. Palmerston's endorsement of the Bonapartist *coup d'état* in France led to his resignation.

1854 Start of the Crimean War.

1855 Palmerston became Prime Minister and resumed general control of foreign policy.

1856 Treaty of Paris ended the Crimean War. Palmerston insisted on stringent terms against Russia.

1860 Garibaldi's campaign initiated a major step towards Italian unity which received the general support of Britain.

1864 Danish Crisis. Palmerston and Russell appeared to offer support to Denmark against Prussia over Schleswig-Holstein but failed to deliver when Denmark resisted.

1865 Death of Palmerston.

Further Reading

There are three biographies which provide valuable information on the three main foreign secretaries of the period. In each case the foreign policy material is part of a general study which includes coverage of domestic issues. However, this can be a useful aid to understanding the wider context in which issues of foreign policy developed and were considered. In each case the most relevant chapters have been identified.

C.J. Bartlett, *Castlereagh* (Macmillan, 1966). See Chapters 5 and 7.

Wendy Hinde, *George Canning* (Purnell, 1973). See Chapters XV (which focuses on the Congress System), XVI, XVII (which deals with the Eastern Question) and XIX.

Jasper Ridley, *Lord Palmerston* (Constable 1970). This tends to blend domestic and foreign policy together within chapters. There are a large number of chapters each of which appears to deal with a very specific topic but which in reality cover wider ground. This can make the book daunting at first sight. However, the extent of detail can make its use very rewarding, especially if the index is used to target limited amounts of information on specific issues and events. When used in this way the volume is actually quite simple to work with.

Textbooks tend to be of limited use for *further* reading since the depth accorded to foreign policy is generally limited. Mostly these are of more use as general *introductory* reading. However the following volume contains a very useful analytical survey:

Norman Gash, *Aristocracy and People* (Edward Arnold, 1979) - Chapter 10 'Safeguard and Security' - this is excellent as a high quality overview of foreign policy in the period 1815-65. Gash makes few if any concessions to the average student but for those willing to make the effort required this is intellectually nutritious fodder.

M.E. Chamberlain, *British Foreign Policy in the Age of Palmerston* (Longman - Seminar Studies series, 1980) This contains a useful opening section on Castlereagh and Canning before proceeding to the main focus on Palmerston.

Index